OPENING CREDITS

CW00434288

Contributors this issue: Simon J. Ballard, Rachel Bellwoar, David Michael Brown, James Cadman, Sebastian Corbascio,, Dawn Dabell, Jonathon Dabell, David Flack, John Harrison, Darren Linder, Brian J. Robb,, Peter Sawford, Aaron Stielstra, Ian Taylor, Dr Andrew C. Webber, Steven West. Caricature artwork for *Cruising* by Aaron Stielstra.

All articles, photographs and specially produced artwork remain copyright their respective author/photographer/artist. Opinions expressed herein are those of the individual.

Design and Layout: Dawn Dabell
Copy Editor: Jonathon Dabell

Most images in this magazine come from the private collection of Dawn and Jonathon Dabell, or the writer of the corresponding article. Those which do not are made available in an effort to advance understanding of cultural issues pertaining to academic research. We believe this constitutes 'fair use' of any such copyrighted material as provided for in Section 107 of the US Copyright Law. In accordance with Title U.S.C Section 107, this magazine is sold to those who have expressed a prior interest in receiving the included information for research, academic and educational purposes.

Printed globally by Amazon KDP

A Word from the Editing Room

Hello and welcome!

Since you're reading this right now, we'd like to thank you for buying the inaugural issue of 'Cinema of the '80s' magazine, a sister publication to accompany the already-established 'Cinema of the '70s' (which will shortly be reaching its seventh issue). We're confident you'll enjoy delving into a smorgasbord of varied and interesting content in these pages, including articles on titles as diverse as *Miracle Mile*, *Fast Times at Ridgemont High*, *Breaker Morant*, *Manhunter*, *Fitzcarraldo*, *The Ninth Configuration* and *The Serpent and the Rainbow* and more. We are also thrilled to include an exclusive interview with Steve De Jarnatt, the director of *Cherry 2000* and *Miracle Mile*.

Both this magazine and 'Cinema of the '70s' grew out of Facebook groups of the same name. We found we had a number of very insightful, knowledgable, passionate and articulate members in the groups and suggested to them the idea of putting together an accompanying print publication. They were eager to be involved. Joining them, we have been fortunate enough to assemble a number of established professional writers with considerable bodies of work to their name. What we've ended up with is a great, eclectic mix of talent - cinephiles and authors bound together by their love of movies. You're holding in your hands right now the result of their collective efforts.

There's something rather great about '80s cinema - the gritty downbeat tone of '70s movies slowly gave way to a slicker, more entertainment-driven style of filmmaking. There's still great storytelling at work in so many of the films we plan to cover, but they are more often than not immediately recognisable and specific in 'feel' to the period. For many of our writers - and, indeed, readers - it's a decade of happy film-going memories, and we hope to capture that joy and magic within the pages of our magazine. Until Issue 2, enjoy!

Dawn and Jonathon Dabell

Remembering William Hurt (1950-2022)

On March 13th, 2022, William Hurt died in Portland, Oregon. He had been diagnosed with terminal prostate cancer and finally succumbed after almost four years battling the disease.

Hurt exploded onto the scene in the 1980s, making a memorable debut in Ken Russell's *Altered States* (1980). His filmography throughout the decade comprised almost one critically and/or commercially successful movie after another. He received three Oscar nominations in consecutive years for his work in *Kiss of the Spider Woman* (1985), *Children of a Lesser God* (1986) and *Broadcast News* (1987), winning the coveted award for the first of those.

He was one of the most consistently excellent actors of his generation.

Hurt's '80s film credits were:
Altered States (1980)
Eyewitness (aka The Janitor) (1981)
Body Heat (1981)
The Big Chill (1983)
Gorky Park (1983)
Kiss of the Spider Woman (1985)
Children of a Lesser God (1986)
Broadcast News (1987)
A Time of Destiny (1988)
The Accidental Tourist (1988)

Rest well, Mr. Hurt. Thanks for the memories.

In Memoriam

**James Caan
(1930-2022)**
Actor, known for *Gardens of Stone* (1987) and *Alien Nation* (1988).

**Bo Hopkins
(1938-2022)**
Actor, known for *Sweet Sixteen* (1983) and *Mutant* (1984).

**L.Q. Jones
(1927-2022)**
Actor, known for *Lone Wolf McQuade* (1983) and *River of Death* (1989).

**Ray Liotta
(1954-2022)**
Actor, known for *Something Wild* (1986) and *Field of Dreams* (1989).

**Nichelle Nichols
(1932-2022)**
Actress, known for *Star Trek II: The Wrath of Khan* (1982) and *Star Trek IV: The Voyage Home* (1986).

**James Olson
(1930-2022)**
Actor, known for *Commando* (1985) and *Rachel River* (1987).

**Paul Sorvino
(1939-2022)**
Actor, known for *That Championship Season* (1982) and *The Stuff* (1985).

**John Steiner
(1941-2022)**
Actor, known for *The Salamander* (1981) and *Cut and Run* (1984).

**Fred Ward
(1940-2022)**
Actor, known for *Southern Comfort* (1981) and *The Right Stuff* (1983).

**David Warner
(1941-2022)**
Actor, known for *Tron* (1982) and *The Man with Two Brains* (1983).

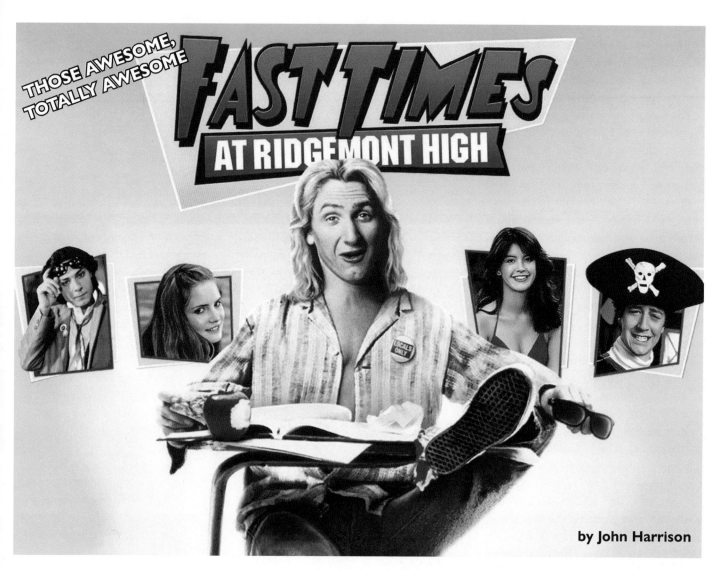

THOSE AWESOME, TOTALLY AWESOME FAST TIMES AT RIDGEMONT HIGH

by John Harrison

For me, the discovery of *Fast Times at Ridgemont High* (1982) is inextricably tied to the multi-platinum 1980 album *Hi Infidelity* by the American AOR (Adult Oriented Rock) band REO Speedwagon. It was early in 1982, the Australian summer still hanging in the air, and I was enjoying something of a gap year, having left high school the year before and deciding to bum around for a year before moving on to university. I had enrolled in a part-time tertiary education course, to help hone a few skills, but my days were spent mostly hanging out with friends at the cinema, record store or video arcade, or locked in my bedroom working on my burgeoning pot-smoking skills, a can of air freshener always at the ready should one of my parents suddenly appear, and enjoying the remarkable new ways in which the magic leaf was able to change my interpretation of some of my favourite music, movies and books.

On the days when I would bother to turn up for my tertiary class, I would usually pull down a couple of quick bongs, grab the Walkman, a few cassette tapes and the latest issue of 'MAD' or 'Creem' magazine to help me pass the 45-minute tram journey there and back. The world of Ridgemont High first entered my life on one

such morning. I was cruising the magazine rack inside the newsagents while waiting for my tram to arrive, when my eyes spied the cover of the September 1981 edition of American 'Playboy'. Bo Derek as Tarzan's mate, Jane, graced the cover. I was not yet of a legal age to buy the magazine, but I had gotten away with it a couple of times before with the middle-aged Italian lady who ran the front counter. Bo was worth the risk, and I made a hasty exit once the lady accepted my five dollars and handed me back my dollar and fifty in change.

Naturally, I wasn't going to draw attention to myself by ogling the Bo Derek layout while riding on public transport, but I figured there was nothing wrong with reading 'Playboy' "just for the articles" while I was out and about. Casting a glance over the table of contents, a piece called *Fast Times at Ridgemont High*, described as a memoir, caught my eye. With the morning's pot now in full effect, I selected *Hi Infidelity* from the handful of tapes I had thrown into my backpack, slid it into the Walkman and pressed play. As the opening electric hum of *Don't Let Him Go* filled my ears, I flicked to page 116. Confronted with a cartoonish, double-page illustration of a blonde, freckled face with braces, about to perform something

5

clearly suggestive on a peeled banana, I settled in to take my first class at Ridgemont High. For me, at that moment in time, *Hi Infidelity* seemed like the perfect aural accompaniment to the story I was reading. *Fast Times at Ridgemont High* was a tale of American high schoolers, and *Hi Infidelity* was a distinctly American album that was being used as the soundtrack to many high school life dramas that very year. *Hi Infidelity* was also an album inspired by, and predominantly about, relationship betrayals and broken hearts, which thematically gelled with what I was reading.

The story published in that issue of 'Playboy' was, I quickly found out, an excerpt of a new book by Cameron Crowe, who was only twenty-two at the time but was already building a reputation as something of a wunderkind writer and journalist, having contributed articles for music publications like 'Rolling Stone', 'Creem', and 'Circus'. With his boyish looks, Crowe was easily able to pass as a high school student and, with the co-operation of the Dean, enrolled as a senior at Clairemont High School in San Diego, spending the 1978-79 school year observing and documenting the people and events taking place around him. The result of that project was 'Fast Times at Ridgemont High', which was first published by Simon & Schuster in September of 1981. The film rights to the book were quickly snapped up by Universal, who wasted no time in fast-tracking the production. While *National Lampoon's Animal House* (1978) is often viewed as the launching pad for the crude teen sex comedy, it was the enormous success of Bob Clark's *Porky's* (1981) which really helped the genre find popularity, with a rash of films like *The Last American Virgin* (1982), *Losin' It* (1983), *Screwballs* (1983) and *Joysticks* (1983), all following in its wake. *Porky's* had paid off big for 20th Century Fox, so Universal were no doubt hoping for the same with *Fast Times at Ridgemont*

High.

The heart of *Fast Times at Ridgemont High* beats around a handful of freshmen and seniors as they start another school year. Nerdy Mark "Rat" Ratner (Brian Backer) is shy around girls and has a major crush on virginal Stacy Hamilton (Jennifer Jason Leigh). While Ratner gets his advice on girls from his best friend, smooth-talking concert ticket scalper and wanna-be ladies' man Mike Damone (Robert Romanus), Stacy receives guidance from her friend Linda Barrett (Phoebe Cates), who presents herself as much more experienced and worldly, and brags of the prowess of her mature boyfriend back home. Stacy's older brother, senior Brad Hamilton (Judge Reinhold) is proud of his position as shift manager at All-American Burger, and is wondering if having a steady girlfriend is going to be a hindrance in his plans to enjoy his last year as a senior

to the full. There is also the perennially stoned surfer, Jeff Spicoli (Sean Penn), whose penchant for lateness, truancy and having pizzas delivered to the classroom when he needs to satisfy the munchies is a constant source of frustration and anger for his history teacher, the authoritative and Hawaii-obsessed Mr. Hand (Ray Walston). As the school year drags on and weekends are spent mostly hanging out or working at the local mall, friendships and loyalties become tested and sexual temptations hard to resist. Spicoli enrages Ridgemont football hero Charles Jefferson (Forest Whitaker) by wrecking his cherished Chevrolet Camaro and blaming it on a rival high school football team, and things turn decidedly darker when Stacy falls pregnant and has to face dealing with the termination completely on her own. We also discover that Linda is not all she presents herself to be, though things perk up for the traditional graduation dance climax, and the familiar closing montage revealing what awaited the main characters in the near-future (the best is given to Spicoli, who it's revealed will go on to save Brooke Shields from drowning, then blowing all the reward money by hiring Van Halen to play at his birthday party!)

With Cameron Crowe adapting the screenplay from his own book, directorial duties went to Amy Heckerling, 28 years old at the time and making her debut feature after helming the short *Getting It Over With* (1980), which she began while a student at the American Film Institute in Los Angeles. Universal Pictures approached Heckerling to direct a film for them after Thom Mount, then president of the studio, was impressed by a screening of *Getting It Over With* that he had attended. After reading through a number of screenplays sent to her for consideration, she eventually settled on *Fast Times at Ridgemont High* as the

film she wanted to do. While Heckerling loved Crowe's screenplay, and felt a genuine connection to the material and an excitement by its potential, she also felt that what she was reading had been watered down by studio directives. After going to the source and reading the novel, Heckerling and Crowe then sat down to work on a revised draft of the script, with the director requesting that several of her favourite moments from the book, which Crowe had omitted in his original draft, be put back into the screenplay.

While *Fast Times at Ridgemont High* may have been marketed as a teen comedy, there was certainly a whole lot more to it than that, something which Heckerling and the cast clearly saw in Crowe's screenplay. For myself, I have always viewed it as something of a sister film to Jonathan Kaplan's *Over the Edge* (1979), an incendiary teen crime drama in which Matt Dillon made his debut. Tonally and thematically, both films are poles apart, but they provide such fascinating yin and yang depictions of American youth on the precipice of great cultural and social change: the drab suburban '70s rock and roll burnouts with nothing to do with their time gives way to the colourful, designer pulse of the emerging MTV generation, where the expansion of the shopping malls meant having much more options for entertainment and social stimulation, not to mention access to more disposable income via all the part-time jobs they offered.

What *Over the Edge* did for Matt Dillon and his career, *Fast Times at Ridgemont High* did for Sean Penn tenfold. In blonde Jeff Spicoli, Penn perfectly encapsulated the classic stoned surfer dude, creating a now-iconic role that will likely forever feature on anybody's list of top ten screen stoners. While the movie is very much an ensemble piece, Penn clearly dominates, and his interactions with Ray Walston's Mr. Hand provide some of its biggest highlights, and many of its funniest scenes. Penn, who had made an impressive film debut the previous year in the acclaimed military drama *Taps* (1981), followed up his performance as Spicoli with another completely different, but no less mesmerizing turn, as an incarcerated juvenile delinquent in Rick Rosenthal's brutal *Bad Boys* (1983). It was a trifecta of performances which laid the foundation for Penn, 21 years old at the time he played Jeff Spicoli, to prove himself one of the finest actors of his generation.

But Penn is just one of several exceptional young actors who appear in *Fast Times at Ridgemont High,* with Jennifer Jason Leigh, Judge Reinhold and Phoebe Cates all putting in terrific and endearing performances in their prominent early roles. Reinhold succeeds in making his largely obnoxious character still endearing and likeable. Leigh had already appeared on episodic television shows such as

FAST CARS,
FAST GIRLS, FAST CARROTS...
FAST CARROTS?

FAST TIMES

A REFUGEE FILMS Production An Amy Heckerling Film "FAST TIMES"
SEAN PENN   JENNIFER JASON LEIGH   JUDGE REINHOLD   PHOEBE CATES
BRIAN BACKER   ROBERT ROMANUS and RAY WALSTON   Screenplay by CAMERON CROWE
Based on the book by CAMERON CROWE   Executive Producer C.O. ERICKSON
Produced by ART LINSON and IRVING AZOFF   Directed by AMY HECKERLING
Read the SIMON and SCHUSTER Book   A UNIVERSAL Picture   Soundtrack available on FULL MOON/ASYLUM Records and tapes
© 1982 Universal City Studios, Inc.

Baretta, Family and *The Waltons* and the slasher film *Eyes of a Stranger* (1981), and she brings a terrific combination of innocence, vulnerability and sexual curiosity to her role as Stacy. Like Penn, Leigh would go on to establish herself as a versatile actor in a range of films which traversed all genres, becoming a cult favourite with audiences and working with directors like David Cronenberg, Paul Verhoeven, the Coen Brothers and Robert Altman, in a career that is still delivering many brave choices and pleasant surprises.

Playing perhaps the most complex character in the film, Phoebe Cates as Linda also provides one of *Fast Times at Ridgemont High*'s most memorable visual moments, when she emerges from Stacy's backyard swimming pool in slow-motion, wearing a red bikini, the top of which she slowly unsnaps while casting a seductive stare at Brad. Of course, it is all just a fantasy which is playing out in Brad's mind, a fantasy which he is masturbating to when Linda embarrassingly walks in on him unannounced. In a 2006 article, 'Rolling Stone' proclaimed this scene "the most memorable bikini-drop in cinema history", and as the '80s wore on, most VHS copies of *Fast Times at Ridgemont High* rented from the local video library would usually start going grainy and developing tracking problems as Phoebe's big moment approached, a sure indication of how many times that segment of the video had been paused, rewound, and rewatched by previous renters. It's certainly an iconic moment in '80s teen cinema, but it shouldn't, and doesn't, detract from the quality of Cates' performance. As she would later prove again, in Joe Dante's *Gremlins* (1984), she had the ability to effectively portray a character that hides her dark secrets, intense anxieties, depression and even possible mental health issues under a veneer of all-American girl wholesomeness.

Elsewhere, other future notables including Eric Stoltz, Anthony Edwards, Nicholas Cage and the aforementioned Forest Whitaker, pop up in smaller supporting parts, all doing their bit to bring some memorable traits to their characters in their limited screen time. Like Rene Daalder's fascinating high school revenge thriller *Massacre at Central High* (1976), adults are rarely part of the world of Ridgemont High. Apart from Mr. Hand, the only adult of any note is biology teacher Mr. Vargas, played by the wonderfully unique Vincent Schiavelli. On something of a grim note, Vargas' statuesque, blonde bombshell wife is played by Lana Clarkson, who in 2003 would be murdered by crazed record producer Phil Spector. Nancy Wilson, guitarist for the rock group Heart and Cameron Crowe's then-girlfriend (and future wife), also shows up in amusing cameo, playing a woman in a car whom Brad thinks is flirting with him, only to suddenly realise she is actually laughing at him because he is still dressed in the ridiculous pirate outfit which his current job requires him to wear while making deliveries.

9

Speaking of music, it forms a vital part of *Fast Times at Ridgemont High*, whether it's Mike Damone trying to scalp Van Halen and Cheap Trick tickets, Pat Benatar lookalikes giving each other competing glances from across the mall or school cafeteria, or the songs that are omnipresent, filling the background through car stereo systems or a shop's PA. Naturally, the film is bolstered significantly by its soundtrack, which serves up an excellent sampler of American AOR and new wave rock, including tracks by the Go-Gos, Don Henley, Donna Summer, Stevie Nicks, Oingo Boingo, and others, and highlighted by Jackson Browne's hit single, *Somebody's Baby*. Heckerling has often talked about the struggles she faced in trying to get the studio to agree to include a number of the more obscure artists, particularly Oingo Boingo, on the soundtrack. Universal initially wanted it to be much more mainstream and completely AOR, while Heckerling was more interested in bands like Fear, Talking Heads and the Dead Kennedys. Eventually, the two parties compromised and agreed to a mixture, which in fact worked out to the film's advantage, as it does create a more realistic representation of what would have really been playing in schools, malls, and on the radio at the time. Issued as a double album, the *Fast Times*

at *Ridgemont High* soundtrack has appeared on CD and vinyl reissue over the years, and is certainly an essential companion piece for any fans of the film.

Heckerling herself is one of the big reasons why *Fast Times at Ridgemont High* succeeds the way it does on so many levels. She understands the characters and the material so well, and knows how to draw natural yet nuanced performances out of her cast. Her terrific work is even more impressive considering it was her debut feature. And while she may have followed it up with two uneven films in *Johnny Dangerously* (1984) and *National Lampoon's European Vacation* (1985), huge commercial success came for her in *Look Who's Talking* (1989) and its sequels, while *Clueless* (1995) would find favour with both audiences and critics. Another coming-of-age teen comedy, *Clueless* saw Heckerling delivering a more updated, female-centric riff on *Fast Times at Ridgemont High*.

Mall culture is another element at the heart of *Fast Times at Ridgemont High*. Next to home and school, it's the place where most of the central characters spend their time,

either working after-school jobs or just hanging out (Mike Damone also finds it a good place to scalp his tickets). Having exponentially risen in popularity during the '60s and '70s, as more and more American families settled out in the suburbs, by 1982 the giant concrete malls had become not just a shopping plaza, but a place for people - primarily teenagers and young adults - to meet, hangout, and be seen. Shopping malls had everything most suburban youngsters needed to keep themselves entertained: food courts, cinemas, video game arcades, bowling alleys, the works. For Ridgemont Mall, the producers used Santa Monica Place for the exterior shots, while the interiors were filmed at the Sherman Oaks Galleria (both still standing but looking much different).

When *Fast Times at Ridgemont High* was sold to US television in the mid '80s, over fourteen minutes of language, nudity and other elements deemed unsuitable for a TV audience were cut and replaced with some extended or alternate scenes to make up the running time. While nothing of an improvement on the original theatrical cut, the TV version can be found as one of the extras on the excellent 2021 Blu-ray release of the film from Criterion and is definitely worth a watch just to see the additional footage (particularly the moments featuring Spicoli, including a rambling but hilarious scene where he recalls how he received a guitar pick from Mick Jagger).

Unfortunately, copies of Cameron Crowe's book are hard to find, and quite pricey when they do surface. Other than the original 1981 hardcover edition, and its 1982 film tie-in paperback, the book has never been reprinted, despite the film's cult status and Crowe's enduring career. Reportedly, the person whom Crowe based Mark Ratner on was someone who thought of the writer as a genuine friend and was upset and disappointed by the book when it appeared, feeling as if he had been betrayed. Feeling remorse, Crowe is said to have prevented any further attempts to reprint the novel. As an interesting aside, the original planned title for Crowe's book was 'Stairway to Heaven: A Year in High School'. The title was inspired by the sense of excitement Crowe felt around the school as a rumoured tour by Led Zeppelin loomed on the horizon. Ultimately, that tour would be cancelled due to the death of Zeppelin's drummer, John Bonham, in October, 1980.

Fast Times at Ridgemont High enjoyed a decent run at the box-office, and even inspired a short-lived 1986 television spin-off called *Fast Times*, which featured none of the original cast apart from Ray Walston and Vincent Schiavelli and has been relegated to well-deserved obscurity (Dean Cameron is no Sean Penn). The movie's subsequent popularity on home video, along with the developing careers of its many stars, helped ensure its cult status. It endures forty years later as a classic and important piece of teen pop cinema. The only thing that could have possibly made *Fast Times at Ridgemont High* any better for me would have been if it had included a number from *Hi Infidelity* on its soundtrack.

"Cleaning up the city... his way!"

DEATH WISH II

by James Cadman

The original *Death Wish* caused huge controversy upon its release in 1974. Audiences crammed into cinemas to see Charles Bronson's character, the liberal architect Paul Kersey, transform into a cold vigilante after a violent break-in leaves his wife dead and his daughter catatonic. Wandering through the dark streets and subway stations of New York City, he looks for opportunities to wipe out the type of lowlifes he blames for wronging his family.

Although not flawless (the police are largely incompetent and the criminals make no attempt to hide their swagger), Wendell Mayes' adaptation of Brian Garfield's 1972 novel holds up as a tough, manipulative thriller. In the final act, with nine muggers dead and a big decline in street violence, the Manhattan authorities are desperate to hide the sharp drop in crime fearing that Kersey's actions will influence others to turn to vigilantism. When Detective Ochoa (Vincent Gardenia) matches Kersey's gun to the killings, he orders him to pack his bags and buy a one-way ticket out of the city. Kersey hightails to Chicago and, upon arriving at the city's Union Station, sees a young woman being hassled by a group of men who cause her to drop her belongings over the floor. Going to her aid,

Kersey looks up at the group as they laugh and gesticulate at him across the concourse. He smiles and makes a gun motion with his hand, taking aim. This simple act is like a wink at the audience, signalling the Paul Kersey we will see return nearly a decade later - a killing machine whose crusades will become more and more far-fetched as the series continues.

Released in 1982, *Death Wish II* is the first of those sequels. Rather than New York or Chicago, the action takes place in Los Angeles. Still working as an architect, Kersey is dating radio host Geri (played by his real-life wife Jill Ireland). As the story begins, we see him spending quality time with his daughter, still left with deep mental scars after being raped and beaten in the first film. Just minutes into the film, trouble flairs up when Kersey, Geri and his daughter attend a street fair. As Kersey queues for ice cream, a gang of thugs (including a young Laurence Fishburne) snatch his wallet. Our man chases them but, after struggling with one of the punks, fails to retrieve his wallet and calmly walks back to re-join the ladies.

Things take a turn for the worse when the giggling gang of muggers find Kersey's address in his wallet and drive to his home where his housekeeper is alone preparing dinner, waiting for Kersey and his daughter to return. The villains smash their way into the house and subject the housekeeper to a prolonged and violent rape (more on that shortly). The gang lies in wait and, when Kersey returns, they knock him unconscious and murder his housekeeper with a crowbar. As if that wasn't enough, they bundle his daughter into a van and drive her to an abandoned warehouse where she too is raped. In a moment of desperation, she jumps through a plate-glass window only to end up impaled on an iron railing. All this happens in the first 20 minutes!

When news of his daughter's death arrives and with no faith in the LA Police Department, Kersey decides once again to take to the streets to avenge her.

My earliest memory of *Death Wish II* was in the '90s - a late-night TV showing of an edited print. As a young teenager, I was struck by the violence and overall nastiness and it still makes for tough viewing 40 years on from its release. Indeed, at the time director Michael Winner (who also helmed the 1974 original) had quite a battle on his hands with censors on both sides of the Atlantic. To achieve an 'R' rating in the US, the distributor Filmways cut parts of the notorious rape scenes while, much to Winner's frustration, the BBFC insisted upon yet further cuts before it was granted a cinema release in the UK. Critics were equally vocal about the "unnecessary" sexual violence and nudity, prompting Winner to respond in an interview at the time that "you can't say what is 'necessary' because there is no necessity in drama." Bronson himself had appealed to Winner to tone down the rape scenes. Rumours later emerged that cinematographer Thomas Del Ruth and his crew walked out in protest at the graphic staging of the rape of Kersey's housekeeper. Although they both receive credit, Richard Kline was brought in to replace him. Del Ruth went on to lens iconic '80s films *The Breakfast Club* (1985) and *Stand by Me* (1986).

Such controversy is not new. More than 20 years before *Death Wish II* appeared, the career of British director Michael Powell never recovered from the backlash heaped on his psychological thriller *Peeping Tom* (1960). Now regarded as a masterpiece, at the time of its release that film was heavily criticised for its voyeuristic depiction of violence and sexual imagery. In the same year, Alfred Hitchcock fell foul of the British censor with his seminal horror *Psycho*. For the now-infamous scene where Janet Leigh is stabbed to death in the shower, BBFC examiners insisted several frames be removed before they grant an 'X'

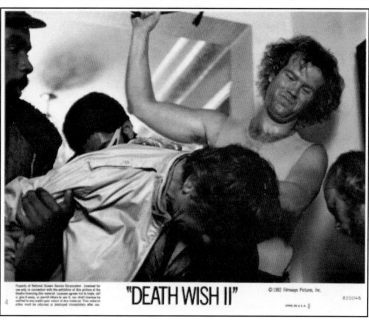

certificate, including "all shots of her breasts or navel" and a reduction in the sound during the attack. In a press conference at the time of the film's release, Hitchcock said: "I am to provide the public with beneficial shocks. Civilisation has become so protective that we're no longer able to get our goose bumps instinctively. The only way to remove the numbness and revive our moral equilibrium is to use artificial means to bring about the shock. The best way to achieve that, it seems to me, is through a movie." The same principle could apply to *Death Wish II*.

Repeating an argument he'd made in 1974, Winner maintained that the extreme violence and gratuitous sexual images were designed to show the true cruelty of the villains and to provoke and validate Kersey's revenge. Interviewed on the set by BBC Film '81, he was keen to emphasise: "The picture doesn't say 'go and get a gun and kill your local mugger.' The picture says 'society has reached this extraordinary point where people are so desperate for law and order that anyone who does this would be applauded'... It shows a mad, prophetic desire to clean up their lives at any cost." In a separate debate, responding to comments made at the time of the film's release, Winner went on to emphasise that he was aware of a "mammoth rise of street violence" since the release of the first *Death Wish* movie. He had a point - violent crime in the state of New York, as a proportion of the population, increased by 33% between 1974 and 1981. During the same timescale in California, the figure was 63%. This very point is established during the opening credits as a radio host quotes the surge in violent and sexual crimes plaguing Los Angeles.

Putting the controversial aspect to one side, *Death Wish II* possesses several qualities that are worth celebrating. On the whole, the action scenes are well-choreographed.

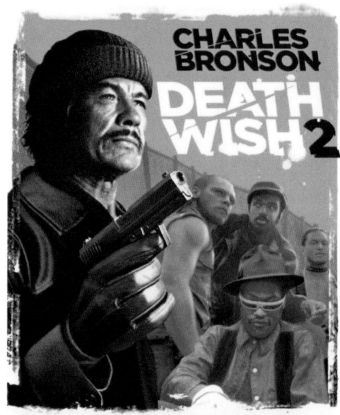

The fight sequences, particularly near the end, are brutal and exciting - especially when we see the gang leader, Nirvana, apprehended by police, and later when Kersey tracks him down to a psychiatric hospital and serves up his own form of rehabilitation. With the exception of a few unhelpful scenes of wobbly dialogue, it is pretty fast-paced and energetic, thanks mainly to its punchy editing (partly executed by Winner under the pseudonym Arnold Crust) and also due to the neat bursts of guitar and synthesiser motifs by none other than Jimmy Page. The soundtrack album, which Page re-released on a limited vinyl press in 2011, has since gone on to be a highly-sought-after collector's item.

Bronson was originally reluctant to reprise the role of Paul Kersey. After refusing to even consider the script, he was eventually lured back with an offer of $1.5 million by producers Menahem Golan and Yoram Globus who had bought the rights to the concept from Dino De Laurentiis. Bronson's on-screen presence is undeniably a huge factor in the film's success. Some critics accused him of sleepwalking through the proceedings. It can certainly be argued that his performance lacks the emotional depth seen in the first film. Screenwriter David Engelbach would no doubt attribute this change to director Winner who rewrote much of his script. Engelbach's original concept had Kersey resisting falling back into becoming what he became, in contrast to the story that made it onto the screen. One plotline Engelbach intended to include was the police claiming that it was Kersey's daughter's mental state that drove her to throw herself out of the window. The suggestion was that, even if they'd found the men responsible, they probably wouldn't charge them with first degree murder, prompting Kersey to give up helping the police, preferring to track them down himself.

The difference this time is that, unlike in the original, Kersey succeeds in avenging his daughter's death by eliminating the very gang that killed her and his housekeeper. The criminals in the first movie never paid for their actions. TV adverts promoting *Death Wish II*'s release proclaimed: "When murder and rape invade your home. When the cops can't stop it, Bronson will - his way!"

Despite some neat exchanges with Detective Ochoa (played again by Gardenia, in a nice nod back to the original), Kersey appears to be void of the morality we saw in the original film. There are a couple of exceptions to this. Shortly after he learns of his daughter's demise, there is a powerful sequence which shows him leaving the city to find peace and solitude in the countryside. We witness his emotion and grief turn into anger and, at that point, there is a stark shift in his behaviour; he gets hold of a gun and we see him equip himself to venture out onto the mean streets of LA. In another, subtle departure from the carnage, Winner has Kersey pause outside churches in the downtown area before appearing to reject their calling. This is affirmed in an ugly scene where Kersey confronts the first gang member. In an abandoned building teeming with rats, Kersey sees the thug grasping a crucifix on a chain around his neck. "Do you believe in Jesus?" Kersey

asks, pointing a handgun at the mugger. "Yes, I do," comes the reply. "Well, you're gonna meet him!" declares the vigilante before shooting him in the chest.

Death Wish II paved the way for three more instalments, all featuring Bronson, with the franchise coming to an end in 1994. The later films, especially *Death Wish 3* (another Winner entry), took on an almost cartoonish feel with Bronson seemingly competing with Stallone for the highest kill count. *Death Wish II* serves as a sort of 'bridge' between that gung-ho excess and the more grounded tone of the original. It was still a huge success, returning double its budget at the US box-office alone and grossing more than $50m worldwide.

For this review, I got hold of an uncut version of the film released in 2017 by an Australian distributor. As well as containing *Death Wish 3*, there is an extra disc which includes three alternative versions of *Death Wish II* - the original theatrical cut (censored to achieve an 'R' rating in the US), the Greek VHS version and the television cut. The latter two contain dialogue and extended scenes that did not appear in the theatrical cut. All versions include a brief written introduction from Bronson specialist Paul Talbot and the TV version uses the 'scene selection' function and subtitles to draw attention to the new and extended footage. It's a great ensemble for fans of Bronson and the popular Cannon era.

THIEF. WARRIOR. GLADIATOR. KING.

CONAN

ON SCREEN

by Jonathon Dabell

The character of Conan was created in the early 1930s by a troubled Texas youth named Robert E. Howard. Howard was strange and socially awkward, with probable mental health problems. He spent the second half of his childhood and all his short adult life living in a town called Cross Plains, Texas, where he worked in several different jobs (all of which he hated). He spent a lot of time wrestling with paranoid delusions that the townsfolk were out to get him, that somehow they were his mortal enemies.

His true ambition was to be a writer, and he spent many hours at his typewriter bashing out stories that were far removed from the mundane tedium of his unhappy existence. These stories were not notably successful during his lifetime and only really achieved the cult status they enjoy today after his death by suicide in 1936. Most were set in fantasy lands created from Howard's vivid and fertile imagination. They appeared in pulp publications like 'Weird Tales', and depicted extraordinary, fantastical adventures - full of action and heroism - written in a colourful, flamboyant prose.

It's no exaggeration to call Howard the creator of the sword and sorcery genre as we now know it. It's very sad that he didn't get to see the influence of his pioneering work within his own lifetime, as witnessing its success might have helped him overcome some of his demons. J.R.R. Tolkien is the other name bandied about when conversations about the "Father of Fantasy Fiction" take place. Tolkien was the one who pioneered detailed world-building and the mythology of his imaginary kingdoms,

but he rarely described action in a detailed way and never resorted to depicting violence. Howard's work contains its fair share of mythology, but his prose focuses on action, violence and heroics within the worlds he created. His characters included the likes of Kull the Conqueror, Solomon Kane and, of course, Conan the Cimmerian. Howard used these characters to escape his real-life misery, living out a happier existence through his writing. Those who knew him said he resembled Conan more than any other character he'd invented in terms of attitude and personality. A tad worrying, perhaps, when you consider that Conan speaks little, fights often, takes whatever he wants, and hacks the hell out of anyone who stands in his way!

An interesting depiction of Howard's professional writing phase can be found in the book 'One Who Walked Alone' by Novalyne Price Ellis (the author's girlfriend for a while). The book was adapted as a film, entitled *The Whole Wide World* (1996), which starred Vincent d'Onofrio as Howard and Renee Zellwegger as Novalyne.

A Conan comic existed long before there was a movie. The first comics were published by Marvel in 1970, written by Roy Thomas and illustrated by Barry Smith. In 1977, the idea of a screen version emerged when producer Edward R. Pressman was viewing a rough cut of the bodybuilding documentary *Pumping Iron*. Surveying the raw footage, Pressman found his attention repeatedly drawn to Arnold Schwarzenegger (a former bodybuilder and multiple winner of the Mr. Universe award). He felt that Schwarzenegger had genuine presence and would probably make a good film star if the right part could be found. He told his friend Edward Summer they should try to think of a project that would be a suitable vehicle for the giant Austrian. Summer was a huge comic book enthusiast as well as a fan of the fantasy-themed artwork by the legendary Frank Frazetta, and he put forth the idea of casting Arnie in a Conan movie. They approached the actor, and he was immediately keen to be involved, little realising it would be five years before a finished product would come to fruition.

Summer and Roy Thomas wrote an early draft of a proposed Conan script, but it wasn't until Oliver Stone got involved that the ball began rolling seriously. Heavily influenced by cocaine, Stone wrote the first full Conan script in "a fever dream" and presented it to Pressman. Stone wanted it to be the first in a potential series of Conan adventures, with the character returning to the screen every year or two for his next big movie, until a dozen or so had been made. He maintains to this day that the studio bosses at the time sold Conan short. He believes they could have developed the adventures into a long-running franchise, like the 007 films, if they'd had more courage and foresight. Pressman and Stone went to London to try to convince directors like Alan Parker and Ridley Scott to helm a screen version of Stone's screenplay, but they were

turned down and, dejected, returned to their hotel to lick their wounds. Stone had heard that prolific producer Dino de Laurentiis was in town, and suggested to Pressman that they should visit the Italian-American movie mogul and sell the script to him and wash their hands of it.

Despite finding the script excessively violent, Dino de Laurentiis found it promising and agreed to buy it. He felt some rewriting would be required before shooting could commence and decided to appoint a director who could carry out the rewrites. He selected John Milius, who had recently co-written the remarkable *Apocalypse Now* (1979) but was smarting after the undeserved box-office disappointment of the excellent surfing drama *Big Wednesday*, which he'd directed in 1978. Milius had little knowledge of the existing Conan mythos, but agreed to come aboard as he felt he could really get his teeth into the project. He launched into extensive redrafting, removing a lot of the magical and fantastical elements from Stone's script so that it became less a fully-fledged fantasy and more an 'Ancient World' picture, a sort of Greek myth or Viking epic transposed to a deliberately undefined period some time between the sinking of Atlantis and the prehistoric era as we know it now. There are still elements of the fantastique - witches, wizards, giant serpents, a bad guy who can transmute into a snake, etc. - but, by and large, the story is set in a time and place that might have been real and feels true to its own code and history.

Also, before shooting a yard of film, Milius approached his old college buddy Basil Poledouris about composing the music. De Laurentiis was keen to use Ennio Morricone, but Milius argued for Poledouris and eventually got his way. Working purely from the script and conceptual storyboards, Poledouris created several rough compositions and sections of score - not whole, finished pieces, but enough to give Milius and the actors a flavour of the bombastic operatic music that would accompany the finished movie.

Milius wanted to get the casting just right. Obviously, Schwarzenegger was ideal as the hulking barbarian, but finding suitable supporting players was essential. For one thing, some seriously big guys needed to be brought in to play the baddies. They needed to look suitably formidable and powerful, or audiences would have a hard time believing Conan was in any real danger. Sven Ole Thorsen, a Danish bodybuilder and strongman competitor, and Ben Davidson, a former line end for a number of NFL and AFL football teams, were cast as Thorgrim and Rexor respectively, the two primary henchmen of the 'boss villain' Thulsa Doom. As for Thulsa Doom himself (a character actually lifted from a Kull the Conqueror story), the great James Earl Jones was hired. With a booming voice that matched his large frame, Jones was perfect for the role. He is given a vaguely otherworldly appearance, enhanced by straightened long-length hair and cobalt blue eyes. We get a real sense that he is the last of a dying superior race. His body language and mannerisms are strange and hypnotic, and there is a cold supremacy, a kind of dominance, about him which makes him a truly formidable foe. He kills calmly, never appearing invigorated or exhilarated by the thrill of combat. When he beheads Conan's mother early on, for example, the mood of the scene feels like some grand prayer rather than an execution.

Sandahl Bergman was chosen to play the warrioress Valeria, Conan's companion and eventual lover, after Milius spotted her in Bob Fosse's *All That Jazz* (1979) and felt she looked like the living embodiment of a Valkyrie. Many actors were screen-tested for the role of Subotai, Conan's loyal sidekick, and Milius soon realised he

THIEF
WARRIOR
GLADIATOR
KING

DINO DE LAURENTIIS
EDWARD R. PRESSMAN
ARNOLD SCHWARZENEGGER · JAMES EARL JONES

CONAN
THE
BARBARIAN

SANDAHL BERGMAN
BEN DAVIDSON
CASSANDRA GAVIOLA
GERRY LOPEZ · MAKO
VALERIE QUENNESSEN
WILLIAM SMITH
MAX VON SYDOW

JOHN MILIUS

was subconsciously looking for someone who resembled his real-life buddy Gerry Lopez, a pro surfer. It then occurred to him to ask Lopez himself to audition, and when the reading went well, the surfer suddenly found himself cast in a key supporting role despite having no prior acting experience (other than playing himself briefly in *Big Wednesday*). Max von Sydow was recruited for the short but pivotal role of King Osric after the original choice Sterling Hayden fell ill. The director didn't think von Sydow would be interested in the role but was surprised when he enthusiastically came aboard. Von Sydow later admitted his son was a massive fan of the Conan comics and had urged him to do it. Last of the main players was the Japanese-born Mako, portraying a wizard who helps Conan and company in their quest. Mako was also asked to do the film's occasional narrated sections. The narration was originally supposed to be spoken by Schwarzenegger, but his accent was a little too thick and, besides, everyone felt the film worked better the less he spoke. So Mako took the task, using his strange, gruffly poetic voice to evoke the impression of a wise old storyteller sitting by a campfire and mesmerising us with tales of high adventure.

The story is one long revenge quest narrative. An opening sequence, directed by the production designer Ron Cobb, introduces Conan as a boy who lives in a snowy mountain village full of farmers, blacksmiths and hunters. He is taught about the power of steel and the might of the sword by his father (William Smith) and nurtured with love by his beautiful, fiery mother (Nadiuska). When the village

is wiped out by a marauding army bearing the standard of the Sect of the Snake, only Conan survives. He is imprisoned and set to work on the Wheel of Pain, a huge corn-grinding machine in the middle of nowhere, pushed in perpetual circles by a number of chained slaves. Years go by and, by the time he reaches adulthood, Conan pushes the wheel alone, now a towering adult of tremendous physical power. He is released from the wheel and sold as a gladiator, and soon proves himself unbeatable thanks to his remarkable strength. He eventually wins his freedom, and sets out on a quest to track down the Snake Cult, hoping to avenge the slaughter of his people, in particular his mother and father.

The quest takes him through many strange cities, landscapes and temples. He picks up companions along the way, like the fighter Subotai, the lethal warrioress Valeria and a slightly comical wizard. They are hired by a desperate old king named Osric whose daughter has been stolen and seduced by Thulsa Doom. The liberation of Osric's daughter is ostensibly the mission they're engaged on, but Conan sees the real prize as his chance for a long-awaited date with destiny, an opportunity to finally face Thulsa Doom.

There are many individually great sequences along

the way, all of them enhanced by Poledouris' incredible operatic score. The opening attack on the village is a thrilling set piece. The Wheel of Pain sequence is a miracle of editing and time lapse (first-night audiences reportedly went wild with excitement as boy-Conan transformed to Schwarzenegger-Conan before their eyes during the Wheel of Pain montage). Similarly splendid is the crucifixion of Conan on the Tree of Woe and his friends' subsequent fight against the demons that come to claim his spirit (a scene stolen directly from the *Hoichi the Earless* segment of the 1964 movie *Kwaidan*). The orgy sequence, where Conan and his companions - smeared in terrifying camouflage - raid a temple to nab back Osric's daughter, is absolutely riveting. And best of all - indeed one of my favourite sequences from *any* movie, *ever* - is the climactic Battle of the Mound (aka 'Two Stood Against Many'), wherein Conan and Subotai take on Thulsa Doom's elite guard at a stone circle in the desert. The sequence is absolutely exhilarating and everything contributes to its effectiveness - the build-up, the music, the editing, the set design, the photography, the stunts, the choreography and, of course, Conan's defiant challenge to his god Crom: "Grant me one request! Grant me revenge! And, if you do not listen, then to hell with you!"

Poledouris' score is exceptional throughout but reaches its absolute zenith in the Two Stood Against Many sequence. This was the first film to make use of the Musync process, which allowed Poledouris to adjust the speed and tempo of his compositions with special editing hardware and software. This meant he could imperceptibly speed up or slow down a piece of music so that certain dramatic booms or beats or gongs were played at very precise moments over the action. This would otherwise have been done by getting the orchestra to painstakingly play the compositions again and again, fractions of seconds different than the time before, to get the right effect. But thanks to Musync, Poledouris was able to complete the job much more accurately and efficiently.

Special mention should be given to stunt co-ordinator Terry Leonard and production designer Ron Cobb, both of whom have brief cameos in the film. Leonard orchestrates some incredible stunts and sword-fights. The Two Stood Against Many sequence looks so real that animal rights activists boycotted the film, incorrectly believing several horses had been injured or killed while shooting it. He also makes the hand-to-hand combat look incredibly visceral and convincing. The final duel between Schwarzenegger and Davidson was carefully rehearsed and performed with real, heavyweight metal swords, something that would never be permitted nowadays. It was remarkably dangerous to perform but the result was worth the risk. Likewise, Cobb's sets and props add immeasurably to the atmosphere and believability of the Conan universe. From relatively simple designs - like the

Sect of the Snake symbol and Conan's Atlantean sword - to massive structures like the Wheel of Pain, the Temple of the Orgy and the Temple on the Mountain, Cobb's work encompasses many indefinable architectural styles and influences, creating a wonderfully immersive fantasy world. And not a CGI moment in sight - we're talking practical effects and hand-built sets all the way, which makes it all feel refreshingly real.

It took several re-submissions to get *Conan the Barbarian* an R-rating. The bloody violence initially earned it the dreaded X-rating, which would have seriously scuppered its box office potential. Even after trims, the violence remains visceral, convincing and exciting though never gratuitous. Despite some surprisingly negative critical reviews, the film was embraced by many critics. And audiences loved it, turning it into a modest hit - not quite a blockbuster, per se, but a very respectable money-maker. Its fan base and cult audience have grown over the years, and it is now regarded as the gold standard of the sword and sorcery genre. And, if you think about it, it's a very distinctive, unique-looking movie. Nothing that came before really has the same singularity of vision and style, and almost everything that came after is either a cheaper-looking knock-off or a production that relies on CGI for its effects.

Conan the Barbarian is, within its genre, a game-changer and a masterpiece.

Happy with his investment, Dino de Laurentiis was keen to get a sequel in motion almost immediately. The studio executives crunched the numbers and felt that if they could tone down the violence enough to secure a PG-rating, the sequel would make millions more at the box office than its predecessor. Comic-book writers Roy Thomas and Gerry Conway came up with a story outline which Stanley Mann fashioned into a script, and the ball was soon rolling on a follow-up.

De Laurentiis knew John Milius would not return for a watered-down Conan entry, despite the director expressing his desire to make a trilogy. Instead, the experienced Richard Fleischer was hired to direct. Schwarzenegger expressed his own frustration at the route the production was taking, feeling that it was a mistake to make a more family friendly Conan pic. He didn't feel the addition of humour really belonged either, with Conan occasionally uttering one-liners and getting drunk, as well as the introduction of a new sidekick, Malak (played by Tracey Walter), who is largely buffoonish and included for laughs.

Ironically, in the UK, *Conan the Destroyer* was considered by the Board of Film Classification as sufficiently violent to warrant a 15-rating (to be viewed by over 15s only), which was exactly the same rating as *Conan the Barbarian*. So, while the PG certification was granted in America, making the film accessible to a greater number of US viewers, this

THE MOST POWERFUL LEGEND OF ALL IS BACK IN A NEW ADVENTURE.

CONAN
THE
DESTROYER

was not the case in every other part of the world.

The plot involves Conan being recruited by the conniving Queen Taramis (Sarah Douglas) to escort a virginal princess named Jenna (Olivia d'Abo) on a search for a fabled horn. Taramis promises to revive Conan's dead lover Valeria if he succeeds, but in reality she plans to have him killed by her Captain of the Guard Bombaata (Wilt Chamberlain) once his usefulness is over. The real purpose of obtaining the horn is to use it to summon the demon-god Dagoth, and part of the ritual of awakening involves sacrificing Jenna (who is unaware of the fate awaiting her) at the exact moment Dagoth stirs. Conan already has a new companion in the clownish thief Malak (a poor replacement for Subotai from the original), but along the way he picks up new sidekicks in the shape of fearsome warrioress Zula (Grace Jones) and a wizard named Akiro (Mako, again though not playing the same wizard he essayed in the earlier film).

The plot structure is a little tedious this time around. The characters ride around a bit, get into a scrape, ride around again, get into another scrape, and so on. Certain critics complained that the first film was excessively violent, serious and doom-laden, and it often seems with this sequel that the makers were too eager to tone down the violence, increase the humour and lighten the tone. Which is all good and well except for the fact that many people *liked* the first film BECAUSE it was serious and doom-laden. Frankly, this sequel plays too much like a live-action cartoon and is worse for it.

It's not entirely terrible, though. Jack Cardiff's photography is pretty good, Poledouris again provides a rousing score (not as majestic as his work on the earlier movie but still rather good) and the production design by Pier Luigi Basile is quite imaginative.

There's a lot more emphasis on magic and monsters this time. One sequence involves a sorcerer who spirits Jenna away to his glass fortress while she sleeps. When the heroes arrive to rescue her, they find the fortress full of mirrors and Conan must wage combat with a mighty monster which is unaffected by blows from his sword (his blade passes straight through the creature as if it is some sort of phantom or shadow). The scene is completely different from anything in *Conan the Barbarian* and feels like it would fit better in something like *Clash of the Titans* (1981) or *The Beastmaster* (1982). It's quite exciting and well-put-together, but it just doesn't feel very 'Conan'.

The casting is generally less effective in this sequel. Schwarzenegger speaks a bit more and, unforgivably, acts silly from time to time. It somehow cheapens him compared to the way he played the character in the first film. Grace Jones is physically impressive but not much of an actress; basketball legend Chamberlain never really convinces as a serious adversary for Conan; Walter is annoying as the comic sidekick; Mako doesn't get much to do; and Olivia d'Abo comes across like a spoilt brat rather than a grand princess who everyone is willing to die for. Sarah Douglas, Pat Roach and Ferdy Mayne have a bit of fun as villainous types, but they play it pantomime-style which isn't as effective as the very serious, chilling approach adopted by James Earl Jones in Part One. Look fast for Sven Ole Thorsen as one of Taramis' guards. He fights Conan in front of a large rock while a frightened Princess Jenna looks on. To ensure audiences wouldn't be confused and think that Thorgrim from the first film has somehow survived, the actor's face is hidden inside a helmet during their big fight sequence, but it's a neat little nod to the earlier movie all the same.

Ultimately *Conan the Destroyer* is Conan-lite and suffers as a result. Some critics, including Roger Ebert and Giovanni Dadomo of 'Time Out', found it an improvement on the original and praised the lighter tone. But most were underwhelmed, and the public never really took to it. It wasn't a flop but it wasn't a hit either, and Schwarzenegger's stint as Conan ground to a halt after just two movies. Time has been kind to the first film, which is now hailed as a classic and looks as good as ever forty years on. The sequel, however, tends to be either plainly disliked or looked upon as a kitsch time-filler for those seeking lightweight fantasy thrills.

One thing is for sure, though. Conan launched Arnold on the road to superstardom, and if it hadn't been for the first movie, he would never have come to dominate '80s action cinema the way he did. Regardless of what certain contemporary critics said, it's a classic. You hear that, critics? And if you do not listen, then to hell with you!

MIRACLE MILE

by Steven West

Miracle Mile? Sounds like an inspirational '80s TV-movie starring JoBeth Williams and Dirk Benedict as the parents of a crippled, plucky nine-year-old who defies all odds by running 1.609km to save his asthmatic little sister. In reality, it refers to the densely populated L.A. district accommodating Museum Row on Wilshire Boulevard, the El Rea Theatre and La Brea Tar Pits, from where the well-preserved remains of mammoths, dire wolves and sabre-toothed cats have been retrieved over the decades. Oh, and it happens to be the title of one of the greatest American films of the '80s.

In 1961, anticipating the title of that most nightmarish of apocalyptic films *Threads*, President Kennedy reminded the world that the existence of every man, woman and child hung by the slenderest of <u>threads</u> thanks to the "nuclear sword of Damocles". Since then, have we ever truly learned to stop worrying and love The Bomb? As recently as April, 2022, CIA Director William Burns suggested that in the midst of Russia's invasion of Ukraine, a desperate President Putin might resort to tactical or low-yield nuclear weapons to fulfil his objectives. Nuclear war is no longer inconceivable. It has become a possibility again rather than something too appalling to contemplate. We can't quite nervously file it away in our collective brain-banks under: "No… they wouldn't, would they?!"

Writer-director Steve De Jarnatt was born a decade before JFK's term. He grew up with 'Duck & Cover' school drills, civil defense from Bert the Turtle, and a presidential campaign by Lyndon B. Johnson where he suggested his warmongering rival Barry Goldwater might trigger

WWIII. The British had something similar, being urged to contemplate 'Protect and Survive' pamphlets (don't forget to label Gran's poisonous, polythene-wrapped corpse) and facing the best-case scenario of a nuclear blast leaving them with third degree burns which would resemble "meat in a butcher's window" (as depicted in a BBC *Q.E.D.* episode called *A Guide to Armageddon*, which simulated a one-megaton nuclear bomb exploding above St. Paul's). The teen variant *War Games* (1983) and numerous opportunistic Italian *Mad Max* knockoffs took the edge off, and by the time the Intermediate Nuclear Forces Reduction Treaty was signed in 1987, the superpowers seemed to agree that such a conflict could not be won and must never be fought. Ronald Reagan had seen *The Day After* (1983) and all was good.

Miracle Mile was among the last significant Cold War nuclear-paranoia movies, preceding HBO's *By Dawn's Early Light* (1990) which was adapted from a novel set in 1991 but published in 1983. De Jarnatt set out in the late '70s to exorcise those old childhood nuclear war demons and Vietnam War-era nightmares, and spent a decade getting the movie made *his* way. It was selected as one of American Film magazine's 'Ten Best Unproduced Screenplays' and, at one point, was optioned by Warner Bros.' production head Mark Rosenberg to appear as a segment in *Twilight Zone: The Movie* (1983) - albeit with a circular, 'it-was-only-a-dream' twist whereby the hero's own literal nuclear nightmare begins afresh at the end.

Ultimately, De Jarnatt spent what he earned as co-writer of *Strange Brew* (1983) to buy back his own script from the

24

studio. He bided his time writing and directing *Man from the South*, a fresh adaptation of a Roald Dahl story for the 1985 pilot of the revived *Alfred Hitchcock Presents* which reunited two of the Master's most memorable blondes, Kim Novak and Tippi Hedren, alongside Melanie Griffith and future *Miracle Mile* actor Danny De La Paz. With Griffith, he made the ambitious, satirical post-apocalyptic *Cherry 2000* (1988), set in 2017 U.S.A. and eventually attracting a HBO-enhanced cult following.

The film he defined as "my life in the '80s" was finally greenlit by John Daly of the Hemdale Film Corporation, whose estimable catalogue of commercially risky projects included another downbeat, Bomb-fearing sci-fi piece, *The Terminator* (1984). Daly nixed De Jarnatt's notion of a romantic closing image of two diamonds coalescing because he believed the picture, budgeted at less than $4 million and encompassing seven weeks of night shooting, should punch its audience in the gut. Beginning in the realm of 'quirky meet cute' and ending with nukes over the Hollywood Hills, the picture was afforded a Tangerine Dream score which, like the film, starts out dreamily romantic before shifting into pounding intensity. The band were a constant in the movie's evolution: De Jarnatt had burned the midnight oil toiling over the script while listening to their *Sorcerer* (1977) score, and temp-tracked his picture with the *Risky Business* soundtrack.

Delivering the catastrophic resolution usually only permitted in mainstream films with a satirical bent (like *Dr. Strangelove* and *Don't Look Up*) and deliberately avoiding the '80s cliches of neon smoke and wet urban streets, the finished picture premiered at Canadian festivals in 1988. It screened at Sitges in Spain (alongside *Society*, *Santa Sangre* and *Vampire's Kiss*) and reached U.S. cinemas by May, 1989. In a week where *Road House* was the highest grossing new film, *Miracle Mile* finished at a lowly no. 15 in the box office charts, behind the lame *Fright Night Part 2*.

By the time of its summer 1991 UK VHS release, terrors of annihilation were calming, and we were nearly a decade on from President Mitterrand's account of preventing the 'unbridled Englishwoman' Thatcher from unleashing an atomic weapon upon Argentina with her "metallic finger." The end of the Cold War was officially confirmed on Boxing Day, 1991, but the terrors so vividly manifested in *Miracle Mile* - like those conveyed in prominent British predecessors *The War Game* (1966) and *Threads* (1984) - were destined to remain undiluted for as long as the world considered nuclear weapons an acceptable deterrent.

De Jarnatt's influences ranged from the novel 'The Day of the Locust' and Cornell Woolrich to, most obviously, Rod Serling's *The Twilight Zone*, which had been resurrected in the mid '80s and articulately conveyed Cold War fears within the framework of a network sci-fi show. Originally conceived as an entirely subjective movie, *Miracle Mile* never leaves the side of its Everyman protagonist, trumpet-

playing nice guy Harry (Anthony Edwards). He remains our onscreen surrogate until The End, even when it may have been prudent, disaster movie-style, to use cutaways to capture the fates of the various colourful characters encountered along the way. Its narrative path is often compared to Scorsese's single-night New York yuppie nightmare *After Hours* (1985), itself taking its name from a *Twilight Zone* episode and thematically linked to other, tonally contrasting 1985 films like the Chicago-shot urban paranoia thriller *The Final Jeopardy* and John Landis' L.A. misadventure *Into the Night*.

Edwards, appearing between his role as the doomed Goose in *Top Gun* (1986) and his long stint as Dr. Green in *E.R.* (1994-2008), deftly pulls off Harry's transition from slightly goofy rom-com hero to the late '80s equivalent of Jimmy Stewart and Cary Grant in a '50s Hitchcock thriller. He falls in love with Julie (Mare Winningham) during a museum walk in the opening title montage, anticipating the harrowing events to come by featuring the first of many onscreen televisions: this one screening a documentary conveying the beginning of life on Earth, in a story set to capture its unambiguous end. The preamble is, depending on your viewpoint, either playful or self-conscious in a way that is now commonplace: Winningham briefly breaks the fourth wall during her character's introduction, glancing directly at the audience - just as Kurt Fuller does at the very end when he looks straight at us/the flash before agonisingly clutching what used to be his eyes.

The romantic backdrop is as 'out of time' as its protagonists. Their love story is built upon old fashioned tropes and pleasures: Harry's voiceover (abandoned as soon as the imminent threat is established), a shared love of old jazz, an affection for the trolley bus that tours the Miracle Mile, a first kiss in glorious Hollywood slo-mo. Winningham relishes the kind of dialogue Bette Davis would have lapped up in the '40s if the Hays Code had allowed it. "Third date Harry," she notes with mischievous glee, "I'm gonna screw your eyes blue." In a further nod to the past, Julie's grandfather - who spends the film reuniting with estranged wife Lou Hancock - is portrayed by John Agar, a major figure in post-WWII monster movies, notably Universal's *Tarantula* and *Revenge of the Creature* (both 1955). The biggest nod to 'Old Hollywood' is the canny use of King Vidor's risqué *Bird of Paradise* (1932), proffering a similarly doomed romance between native Dolores Del Rio and outsider Joel McCrea on the South Sea island where both are destined to meet a premature end.

The plot hook is a now anachronistic personal nightmare: what if you happen to answer a ringing payphone and discover something disturbing you weren't meant to know? The wrong-place-at-the-wrong-time contrivance makes De Jarnatt's story a contender with Antonio Mercero's Emmy-winning *La Cabina* (1972) - itself playing like a one-off Spanish *Twilight Zone* - for most frightening telephone booth sequence of all time. Other fateful coincidences abound: Harry's decision to quit smoking as his love life flourishes unwittingly triggers a Rube Goldberg-esque chain of events: his discarded butt is taken by a bird to its nest, and the resulting fire takes out power lines, so he unintentionally stands up his promising date. Like an apocalyptic *High Noon*, and a forerunner of TV's *24* (itself fond of nuclear threats), onscreen ticking clocks remind the audience that the events are unfolding in real time from the point at which Harry wakes up late. Incidental portents of doom include a panicky Harry hitting a palm tree, releasing a deluge of rats on his bonnet - a possible nod to L.A.'s prominent position in the 'Rattiest American City' charts.

As a barely coherent homeless dude provides post-midnight L.A. colour, Harry answers the phone outside Julie's diner workplace: it's the world's worst 'Wrong Number'. A near-hysterical missile silo worker, with the all-American name Chip, brings the news everyone fears: "We're locked in… we shoot our wad in 50… we'll get it back in an hour and ten…" Chip is swiftly executed, his authentic terror superseded by an emotionless superior whose demeanour and advice echoes that of the pod people in Don Siegel's endlessly influential Cold War chiller *Invasion of the Body Snatchers* (1956): "Forget everything you've just heard and go back to sleep." The frantic Chip is portrayed by Raphael Sbarge though, tantalisingly, Crispin Glover submitted a 20-minute audition for the tiny yet essential role.

L.A. at the (possible) end of the world is distilled to the disparate collection of diner regulars, arguing over the existential threat and re-enacting the centrepiece of Hitchcock's *The Birds* - a film released in the U.K. a month prior to the Cuban Missile Crisis of 1963. De Jarnatt, like Hitchcock, finds humour in our darkest hour, from the relatably comic interaction between the patrons to the recognisably human slapstick of a shaken Harry walking into the diner's glass door after the call. Before we all became enslaved to the high-powered computers in our pockets, *Miracle Mile* repeatedly positions humans behind glass and in front of screens, adding to the fishbowl sense of voyeuristically watching ordinary folk caught up in a universal nightmare.

The attention to detail includes stockbroker Denise Crosby reading Joseph Pinchon's 'Gravity's Rainbow' (1973), an iconic combination of existential dread, political satire and cock jokes that climaxes with a rocket frozen in time above the (fictional) L.A. theatre The Orpheus. In our era of anti-vaxxer keyboard warriors and climate change deniers, a grim familiarity now adorns the split societal response to Harry's talk of imminent destruction. A fake flight attendant (wearing her sister's outfit) shares her nuclear war nightmares. Harry is reminded how many

There are 70 minutes to the end of the world.
Where can you hide?

MIRACLE MILE
The Ultimate Thriller

good insomniac actors there are in this town. A tarot card reader sleeps through the whole thing. The chef acts on impulse, firing a gun in the air and fleeing with a trolley full of cans. Transvestite Roger (Danny De La Paz), the first of the story's LGBTQ+ characters whose sexuality is neither patronised nor over emphasised, appears nonplussed.

This microcosm of humanity in its last days, true to form, spends its final hour or so indulging in futile debate. Disagreement about what constitutes a safe refuge, as if it were credible to head to the South Pole before the strike. Someone asks if there are any Christians in the group. In the AIDS era, another notes that condoms won't be needed. Conversation surrounding essential people to bring along produces suggestions of MENSA ("That's not a person, it's an organisation"), Dr. Joyce Brothers and Harry Belafonte.

We never see this eclectic bunch again once Harry's search for Julie becomes a frantic mission based on the assumption the threat is real. The fast-moving, episodic narrative structure perfectly suits his plight, while diverting vignettes include encounters with a post-*Aliens* Jenette Goldstein, Brian Thompson as a gay bodybuilder and a young Mykelti Williamson. The latter portrays a doomed, stereo-hawking thief caught in a racially charged encounter with a pre-*Reservoir Dogs* Eddie Bunker as a nightwatchman at an exploding gas station, anticipating devastating real-life things to come in the city. De Jarnatt once noted how people felt the film to be over-the-top until the L.A. riots. Middle-of-the-night citizens default to the emergency

human setting of "everyone for themselves", collectively losing their shit.

There's a remarkable moment in which Harry, instigator of a chain reaction of carnage in a city only needing a sufficient trigger to descend into anarchy, fleetingly wonders if the phone call might have been a hoax. He considers the chance he may have caused unwarranted mayhem on Wilshire Boulevard by broadcasting an unverified pending disaster. As the sun rises and the time of the expected attack appears to pass, the denizens of 'civilised' Western society fight and fuck in the streets, loot stores, set cars on fire, trample corpses underfoot (one of them, amusingly, clutching 'Variety'), pointlessly create traffic jams and shoot off their guns because they can. If the film culminated in a reveal that the phone call was a scam, the movie would remain a potent, misanthropic tract, a late 21st century equivalent to *The Twilight Zone*'s 'The Monsters are Due on Maple Street', in which American suburbia swiftly succumbs to its barely contained existing paranoias and prejudices once modern luxuries cease to function.

The reality of worst-case scenario is confirmed via a horrifying echo of Ed Zwick's authentic TV anchor-men and women reporting on an escalating crisis in the outstanding *Special Bulletin* (1983). Here, we witness (while many ignore) a live broadcast on the TV screens of a window display in a shop subsequently smashed to pieces. A cameraman is gunned down on live television, the panicking host alluding to "unconfirmed rumours."

Few denouements in '80s cinema are as impactful as *Miracle Mile*'s final, heart-breaking ten minutes, designed as a series of increasingly ominous opening doors for its reunited couple. Julie's last-minute optimism provides a glimpse of humanity at its best: she assumes survivors will help each other and rebuild. Harry, our Jimmy Stewart for the 'Greed is Good' era, has seen Los Angeleans in a crisis and confirms: "It's the insects' turn". Kurt Fuller's Gerstead, the last person they encounter, is our species at its worst: facing The End by hoovering up every available drug, caught apparently raping a corpse and ranting: "I could be out fucking penguins with Jacques Cousteau!" as America comes under attack. His final act? One of Trumpian stupidity, looking directly at the nuclear flash.

Harry and Julie overcome the film-long romantic comedy dilemma of getting back together on their fraught first (and last) night. The story comes full circle, back to the tarpits, into which they gradually sink during their last moments on Earth as a flesh and blood couple, speculating about being found together in whatever remains of them and the planet, perhaps ending up in a museum like the one at which they met. There aren't many great cinematic love stories that conclude with the lovers descending into oblivion but then, there aren't many films that can make the following line sound like one of the most romantic

exchanges in movie history: "Maybe we'll get a direct hit. It'll metamorphosise us."

In a sensible universe - perhaps one without extinction-bringing weapons in the hands of rich, unstable white men - *Miracle Mile* would have proved a lucrative calling card for its writer-director. While the picture has, at least, enjoyed a decent afterlife thanks to Blu-ray special editions and retrospective critical love, De Jarnatt has kept busy as a novelist with occasional delves into network television, reuniting with Anthony Edwards for two episodes of *E.R.* (1998-99), including the Halloween-set *Masquerade*. *Miracle Mile* is his greatest achievement, and it continues to haunt us far more than any lavish disaster movie, be it the gleeful ravishing of Wilshire Boulevard in Mick (*Threads*) Jackson's faintly satirical *Volcano* (1997) or the terror of Matt Reeves' *Cloverfield* (2008). The latter was ostensibly a remake of *Miracle Mile* with a location shift to New York, plus a Godzilla-inspired monster and more-or-less the same ending. But, crucially, no Harry and Julie.

Fans of *Miracle Mile* are encouraged to check out SCRAM, an album by the band Head Noise from South Wales. It is described by the group as "post-apocalyptic synthpop." The album has an 80's flavour and even contains a track called *Miracle Mile* (https://www.youtube.com/watch?v=CeITmPdahX8).

An Interview with Steve De Jarnatt

UCLA Archives.
Photo courtesy of Steve De Jarnatt

Dawn Dabell speaks to the multi-talented Steve De Jarnatt about his '80s film work. Steven West's in-depth article on *Miracle Mile* (1988), which De Jarnatt wrote and directed, can be found on page 24.

DD: We'd like to talk a bit about your career in the '80s. But first, let's start specifically with *Miracle Mile* because it's been covered in the magazine by one of our writers, Steven West.
As someone who was born in the early '50s, presumably you grew up in an era when the nuclear threat was a constant concern. Did that childhood awareness of potential nuclear annihilation shape your imagination? It must've been crazy to be so young yet taking part in 'Duck and Cover' drills so you'd know what you were expected to do in the event of a nuclear attack! What was that like? And was any of that in your mind when *Miracle Mile* was being written?

SDJ: Essentially, writing *Miracle Mile* and spending a decade getting it made was my personal exorcism of the terrible nuke dreams I had growing up. I was raised in Longview, a little logging town in Washington State. It was in the shadow of Mt. St. Helens where my summer camp was. They made plutonium up the Columbia River in Hanford. Just 7 miles to the south was the Trojan Nuclear Plant. I had a recurring dream where I would be in a park on a beautiful sunny day. Then it would suddenly get darker, not from clouds, and out on the horizon were dozens of bombers with the arc of missile vapor trails behind them. One bomber would swoop down and nearly blot

the sky as fire leapt out of the ground and witches began to fly around, cackling. I'd be frozen. I was laying on my back, unable to move as the bomber stopped overhead. The bomb bay doors opened and, in slow motion, a giant Fat Boy began to fall towards me, right for my nose. The missiles flew over, dozens of them, exploding in the distance and a forest of mushroom clouds grew up towards the heavens. Then the shock wave came. Ever since I made the film, I no longer have the dream. I gave it to others, I guess!

DD: I understand your script for *Miracle Mile* was considered one of the best unproduced scripts circulating Hollywood from as early as 1983. Is that true? I wonder, did it ever get close to being made before 1988, and if so, were any other directors attached to it, or was it always destined to be your 'baby' if and when the time came to make it?

SDJ: I dropped out of AFI in the mid '70s. in my class were John McTiernan, Ed Zwick, Marshall Herskowitz, Ron Underwood, Rick McCallum and Stuart Cornfeld (producer of *The Fly, The Elephant Man, Tropic Thunder* and others). Marty Brest and Amy Heckerling were in the class ahead of me.
I spent two years "willing" a short film into being. *Tarzana*. It

was shot in 35mm in B&W with old Mitchell BNC cameras, Cooke primes, slow Plus X stock, and John Alton-style noir lighting. Even though it was barely a student film, with a budget of $8k to start, I somehow assembled a dream cast of Eddie Constantine, Timothy Carey, Charles Knapp (the coroner in *Chinatown*), Kate Murtaugh (the madam in *Farewell, My Lovely*), Reni Santoni (from *Dirty Harry* and *Bad Boys*), Edie Adams, Ann Dusenberry (*Cutter's Way*) and my AFI classmate Carel Struycken (the giant from *Twin Peaks*) in his first role. The lead was the private eye, played by Michael C. Gwynne.

We shot it four times with three different DPs (the same gaffer, though) over two years. When it played at Filmex (the biggest festival those days, on a par with Sundance today) as the opening short accompanying Marty Brest's featurette *Hot Tomorrows*, I went from being a busboy to a Hollywood director literally overnight. Everyone in town had come to see Marty's film and the next day twelve agents called to sign me.

I turned down 30+ offers to direct films. I was a snotty little auteur even though I was broke, but producer Tony Bill took me to Warner Brothers who were interested in developing something for me to do. I pitched the basic nutshell of *Miracle Mile* and they paid me Guild minimum to write it.

I turned it in in the December of 1979, and they loved it. I was always set to be the director (I had more 'heat' in town as a would-be helmer at that point), but they wanted to put more writers on it. I asked for it back. They obliged, which would be pretty rare today. I had a free year of turnaround, then had to option it a few times. After a couple years I could either buy it back outright or someone else could.

Meanwhile, Joel Silver had sent my scripts up to Rick Moranis and Dave Thomas who were looking for someone to work with them on a Bob and Doug McKenzie film called *Strange Brew*. I got hired. We knocked around some ideas (they were going back on SCTV and needed someone to blast out a draft for MGM to give a green light to). I wrote *Strange Brew* in 10 days. They hired me to direct but in the end, it went as a Canadian points production, and I was paid 50k NOT to direct (good work if you can get it!) I gave every penny to Warner Brothers, just before the deadline, and owned my baby [the *Miracle Mile* rights] unencumbered once more.

The first time 'American Film Magazine' ever did a "Ten Best Unproduced Scripts in Hollywood" list, where they had pretty much every script in Hollywood history, *Miracle Mile* got

chosen as one. That upped the heat again and Warner Brothers head Mark Rosenberg (brother of Alan, who played the Young Streetsweeper in the film) decided he wanted it back as the basis for *Twilight Zone: The Movie*. I got offered $400,000, maybe more, to sell it back and

Photo courtesy of Steve De Jarnatt

31

stevedejarrnatt.net
Photo courtesy of Steve De Jarnatt

to not direct. The only major change they wanted was that Harry wakes up at the end and discovers it was all a dream, then it starts happening all over again for real. I think I said if George Miller (right after *The Road Warrior*) wanted to do it, I'd cave in. But I was told it was unlikely he'd even look at it, so I spent the rest of the decade getting it made myself. I changed one aspect of that first draft, which had an older Harry finding himself back in LA after 15 years. When he gets the phone call, he barges in on his ex and kid (that reconciliation theme was transposed to the grandparents for the filmed version).

DD: The casting in *Miracle Mile* is particularly interesting. You need a very specific kind of actor to carry off something so offbeat, so off-kilter and quirky; something that's very dark on one hand, yet grimly humorous and romantic on the other. Talk me through the casting process, how you ended up with these particular actors (who are all just perfect, by the way).

SDJ: Well, there were some near productions involving Nic Cage and Kurt Russell (and even Paul Newman in the 'older Harry' version). But after *Top Gun*, Tony Edwards had 'heat' and he was the perfect Harry, our closest thing to a modern Jimmy Stewart. Mare Winningham and he knew each other, and we both went to bat for her. John Daly of Hemdale (the company that financed it) finally gave us a green light.

The supporting cast were all some of the best actors around. It was amazing to get them and rehearse in the diner, etc. (see the Kino Lorber Blu-ray extras for the reunion at Johnnie's Coffee Shop, etc).

DD: There are several films from that period which deal with an impending or already-happened nuclear catastrophe - *The Day After*, *Threads*, *War Games*, *When the Wind Blows* and *By Dawn's Early Light* spring to mind. There are people who consider *Miracle Mile* the best of the lot - it even appears on the 'Rolling Stone' list of best films of the '80s. That must make you very proud, yes? And to extend that question, if we take *Miracle Mile* out of the equation, which of those other titles is your personal favourite within this genre and why?

SDJ: Well, even though I wrote it in the '70s and was hoping for it to be the very first film to come out and shake up a complacent world, *The Day After* certainly helped us. It showed there was a huge audience for the subject for one thing. I still haven't seen *Threads*, which

I am told is the best ever. I didn't want to be influenced, so I didn't see it. *The Last Wave* (1977) was somehow an influence too, I'd say.

DD: Another of your '80s films was *Cherry 2000* - your big screen directing debut, in fact! How did that come about?

SDJ: I was getting ready to make *Miracle Mile* with Nic Cage on a 2-million-dollar budget. John Daly was doing the banking in Holland. Nic was turning down everything after *Valley Girl* made him bankable.

I had a 3-picture deal with Orion. Mike Medavoy, the head of the studio and fan of *Tarzana*, called me up and said: "I'm sending you a script [*Cherry 2000*] and you gotta do it."

I said: "Nic is turning down everything. Daly is still getting the *Miracle Mile* money in the bank. So, OK, send it!"

Then, an hour later, I got a call from Barry Hirsch, one of the biggest lawyers in town. He was representing Francis Ford Coppola and Nic Cage who were set to make *Peggy Sue Got Married*. Barry said to me: "Look, kid, Nic is gonna do *Peggy Sue* and a couple of other films. Then we'll slot your little film in, in a year or two…"

I said: "Let me talk to Nic." Hirsch said: "He's on Catalina without a phone. That's the way it is."

I tried to get hold of Nic. Everywhere the message was "I'm on Catalina without a phone!"

So, I called up Medavoy later that day and said: "Send me the script!"

I read about 20 pages of *Cherry 2000* and thought it was weird and great. Right up my alley. I committed to direct the film. After about a week, I heard from Nic who admitted he'd been letting his attorney do a bluff to see if we'd delay. That's all it was, a bluff. He asked if we could delay, but I had to tell him I was on another show now for a year at least.

That was that.

DD: One of my favourite aspects of *Cherry 2000* is the score by Basil Poledouris. He's one of my favourite composers - a genius! His *Conan* soundtrack is just extraordinary. He's greatly missed. What was it like to work with him? And while we're on the subject, I may as well ask about your experience of working with the legendary Tangerine Dream too (who scored *Miracle Mile*).

SDJ: Basil is the best. As a person and composer. After turning down all these features to direct - from 1978 to '85 - I finally actually did direct something just before *Cherry 2000*. A portion of the '80s reboot of *Alfred Hitchcock Presents*. It was a four-part TV-movie and I got to do the famous *Man from the South* episode. The original starred Steve McQueen and Peter Lorre. Again, somehow, I was fortunate to assemble an amazing cast: John Huston, Kim Novak, Tippi Hedren, her daughter Melanie Griffith, Steven Bauer, etc. It turned out really great and became a

series. Basil scored that. Though we did meet with Frank Zappa (who wanted to score *Cherry*), we were really lucky to get Basil's genius work. I think the things that make *Cherry* work and have charm are the score, the costumes by the brilliant Julie Weiss, and the supporting cast.

On Tangerine Dream, I wrote the script for *Miracle Mile* while blasting their first score, *Sorcerer*, all night. When we'd assembled the rough cut (with some Tangerine Dream temp music), we sent it to them as a lark. They'd been the hottest soundtrack team in the '80s. Somehow, they loved it! The original founder Edgar Froese and a new young protégé Paul Haslinger worked on the *Miracle Mile* score. I got to go over to Vienna to work with them - pure bliss! The film wouldn't even work without that magical score.

DD: You worked with some fine actors in the '80s, many of them at the dawn of their career and a few well-established old-timers. Melanie Griffith, Laurence Fishburne, Ben Johnson, Anthony Edwards, Mare Winningham. Does anyone from that list - or perhaps someone I've missed - stand out as an absolute dream to work with?

SDJ: Tony and Mare. Just the best. Our schedule was so tight. We shot all night for seven weeks. We were trying to make a 25-million-dollar film for 3 million dollars. I'm not sure how we ever did it, but we were all very prepared. As you may know, Tony and Mare - after each having other marriages and many children - are now together. They're married to each other. Diamonds! If nothing else, my film had some small part in that wonderment.

DD: Do you prefer to direct films you've written yourself, or do you prefer directing something written by someone else? *Cherry 2000* is an example of the latter and *Miracle Mile* an example of the former - I wondered which approach, if any, was more personally satisfying and preferable to you?

SDJ: Ideally conceived, written and directed by me. *Cherry 2000* was a different experience, as the film was already in motion (they were desperate to hire me because Irvin Kershner had just dropped out). As much as I'd tried to prep, the sets weren't always ready, the weather misbehaved, and filming in every toxic location in Nevada was really a chore. I'm glad people dig it today, but it was a tough one back then and made virtually no money.

DD: I'm sure our readers would be fascinated to know what you consider the greatest film of the '80s? (Feel free to pick one of your own if you like!)

SDJ: In no particular order, and forgetting many I'm sure, I'd pick:

The Road Warrior, Blue Velvet, Blade Runner, Do the Right Thing, Come and See, Heathers, This Is Spinal Tap, Robocop, Raising Arizona, The Terminator.

And the greatest film of all time - *Mac and Me*.

DD: Thanks so much for taking the time to talk to me.
SDJ: My pleasure. If anybody wants to check out what I am doing creatively these days, I have mainly been writing fiction. I have a book of award-winning work out now, called 'Grace for Grace' (some of the stories have been selected by The Best American Short Stories). It is available in print on Amazon, or via this link (https://press.uchicago.edu/ucp/books/book/distributed/G/bo50634192.html) on University of Chicago Press. I think there is a 20% discount if you use the promo code PRDEJARNATT.
It's also available as an Ebook.

Thanks for the support!

"Shoot Straight, You Bastards"
BREAKER MORANT .vs. THE BOER WAR

by Peter Sawford

War has been a good source of material for filmmakers through the years. Both World Wars, the Korean War and the conflict in Vietnam have been the subject of a substantial number of films. Very few, though, have been made about the Boer War. *Breaker Morant* (1980) is one of the exceptions.

Set in 1902 during the last years of the Second Boer War, *Breaker Morant* deals with the arrest and court martial of three soldiers from the Bushveldt Carbineers (an Australian unit serving under the British Army). The three men, Lt. Harry 'Breaker' Morant (Edward Woodward), Lt. Peter Handcock (Bryan Brown) and Lt. George Witton (Lewis Fitz-Gerald) are accused of murdering Boer prisoners and a German missionary. Major James Thomas (Jack Thompson) is given the task of defending them, but it soon becomes clear there's more to the trial than the pursuit of justice. The three men have become pawns in a deadly game of world politics.

In February, 1978, the stage version of *Breaker Morant* was performed for the first time by the Melbourne Theatre Company. Written by Kenneth G. Ross and directed by John Sumner, it brought to light a chapter of Australian military history that few people knew about. Although it didn't meet with huge critical acclaim, the movie rights were quickly snapped up.

Director Bruce Beresford, born in Sydney in 1940, had been making movies since his teens but had encountered problems trying to break into the top tier of the industry despite trying his luck in both the UK and Nigeria. Back in Australia, early directorial attempts such as *The Adventures of Barry McKenzie* (1972) and *Barry McKenzie Holds His Own* (1974) - both starring Barry Humphries - had been decent box office successes but didn't lead to the influx

of offers Beresford hoped for. He was on the lookout for a project which would interest him and possibly pave his way to the big time when he first saw Ross' play. Realising its potential, Beresford spoke to Ross about turning it into a film and then sought finance from the Australian Film Commission. Beresford understood the play was very strong. Along with collaborators Jonathan Hardy and David Stevens, he wrote the screenplay with the stage version still very fresh in his mind, expanding the action to shake off some of its stage-bound roots.

Despite his relative lack of experience, Beresford was given virtual *carte blanche* as far as casting was concerned. Terence Donovan had performed admirably in the stage play but Beresford decided not to use him as Morant in the film, casting him in the role of Captain Hunt instead. Beresford opted to offer the title role to Edward Woodward. The director had seen a photo of the real Morant and been immediately reminded of Woodward. He pushed ahead with casting him despite the reservations of the Australian Film Board (who weren't convinced that financing a film with a Brit as a central Australian character was a sensible idea). An experienced, talented and well-respected actor on stage and screen, Woodward was probably best known for starring in Robin Hardy's *The Wicker Man* (1973) and his recurring role as Callan in the series of the same name which ran on British television between 1967-72, winning him a Best Actor BAFTA in 1970.

For the role of the irrepressible and eternally chipper Lt. Handcock, Beresford turned to fellow Australian Bryan Brown with whom he'd worked on *Money Movers* two years previously. A mainstay of Australian theatre, Brown had appeared in a number of films in mainly small roles, but Lt. Handcock would propel him to international

35

recognition. Lewis Fitz-Gerald, a virtual unknown, was cast as the youngest of the three defendants while veteran Australian actors Charles Tingwell and Vincent Ball were added as Lt-Col. Denny, the officer in charge of the court martial, and Col. Hamilton, a man left to do the dirty work when his superiors wash their hands of it.

The only actor the Film Commission insisted must be given a prominent role was Jack Thompson. Originally offered the role of Handcock (which he refused, then later accepted), Thompson eventually ended up playing Major Thomas, the officer given the unenviable task of defending the accused (John Hargreaves was originally offered this part but was forced to drop out).

Breaker Morant is mainly set in the courtroom and around the prison where the three are being tried. The events described during the trial are shown in flashbacks. The film also shows the political and military machinations going on at the homes of the commanding officers that will eventually doom the men no matter what.

Woodward takes centre stage from the word go. While never hogging the limelight or attempting to steal scenes from the others, he's the rock at the centre of the film. Morant was a difficult man in real-life by all accounts, an adventurer who travelled far and wide and worked wherever he could, gaining his nickname as a 'breaker' of horses in the Australian outback. A wannabe poet, he was

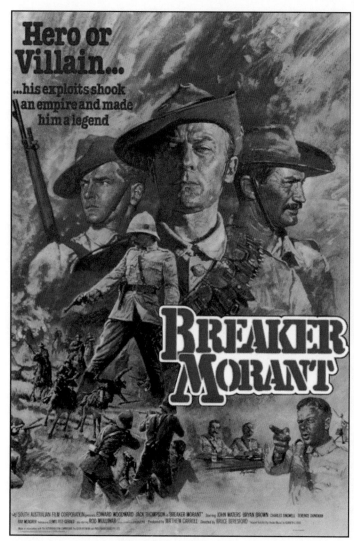

the archetypal barrack room lawyer who, despite his rank, was always ruffling feathers and upsetting those stationed above and below him. Woodward plays him as a slightly cold and distant person who makes friends infrequently but, when he does, shows total and unshakeable loyalty toward them. Throughout the trial, he often clashes with the prosecuting council Captain Bolton (Rod Mullinar) and shows flashes of temper. When asked under what order they shot the prisoners, he angrily responds: "Rule .303. We caught them and shot them under rule .303!" Woodward brings an air of restraint to Morant which makes his occasional outbursts in court all the more surprising. Chided by Major James, he admits that it's very un-British to display such an eruption of emotion. Morant is the most fatalistic or, depending on your point of view, most realistic of the accused men. He hopes that justice may prevail, that freedom may still come his way, but deep down he knows they've been dead since the moment they were arrested and he's already made peace with his destiny.

Handcock shares some of Morant's pessimistic outlook, but at the same time hopes that perhaps they'll get off or just end up in prison and he'll still get home to see his wife.

Handcock is the sarcastic, witty member of the trio - the archetypal Ocker. Always ready with a sardonic quip or biting remark, he's the source of much of the film's humour. Brown plays him as a happy-go-lucky character, clearly bored by life at home, who's joined the army looking for adventure but ended up facing the possibility of standing before a firing squad. He's achieved his rank through hard work, but one senses there is still an ingrained dislike of authority which has never been completely subdued in him, a mistrust toward those who have gained equal rank through money, influence or straightforward crawling. In many ways, Handcock is also the most honest of the trio. He knows what he's done, is content that he's done his duty and, although aware his actions have brought him to where he is, doesn't necessarily agree that fate has dealt

that Handcock did indeed kill the missionary and that his friends are not entirely falsely accused, but he's quickly reminded of the brutal facts of the situation they're in. Fitz-Gerald gives Witton a slightly naïve, simplistic outlook on life - if you do as you're told and tell the truth, no harm will come to you. But as the film rolls on, this façade is slowly broken down and he comes to realise the world isn't always fair and that telling the truth isn't always the safest option. Morant and Handcock show almost fatherly affection towards him as they try to preserve his inner goodness and protect him from a world that decided their lives, or more properly deaths, will serve a higher political purpose. On more than one occasion, both Morant and Handcock look at each other with raised eyebrows before introducing Witton to yet another of life's inequities. His

him an unfair hand. Brown seems totally at home with the character and most of what Handcock says seems to come naturally thanks to the actor's easy-going, laidback style.

Over the course of the film, the friendship between Morant and Handcock becomes stronger by the day. In the final sequence we believe that neither man could wish to have a finer friend and comrade by his side. They are willing to hold up their hands and admit to some wrongdoing. Lt. Witton is different, in the sense that he is green and slightly raw, and believes in the job they're doing and in the righteousness of the British Empire. He believes he's done nothing but his duty, and endlessly professes himself innocent of all the charges and transgressions levelled against him. Witton is furious when he finds out

unworldliness to the perils of their situation is never better illustrated than when he asks if they're likely to have a prison sentence or be cashiered. He is shocked when Major James tells him he's being tried for a capital offence. Fitz-Gerald only had a few performances on Australian television before Beresford plucked him from virtual obscurity for this role, but given the strength and depth of his performance, you'd never know it. He more than holds his own alongside his two more experienced co-stars.

Charles 'Bud' Tingwell was probably best known to British audiences as the eternally exasperated Inspector Craddock in the Margaret Rutherford 'Miss Marple' films. Here, he plays Lt-Col. Denny, who clearly has orders to see to it that, no matter what Major James says or what

evidence is presented, the result must never be in doubt. Tingwell is resolute and unbending in what he sees as his patriotic duty, his belief that sacrifices must be made for the greater good. Denny has a path he's been told to walk, and nothing is going to stop him from walking it. Like Tingwell, Vincent Ball served in Britain during WW2 as part of the Royal Australian Air Force and, after deciding on an acting career, soon found work in such diverse fare as two Carry On films, *Where Eagles Dare* and the TV series *Crossroads* where he took over the role previously played by non-other than Charles Tingwell! Ball is perfect as Col. Hamilton, the man left by Kitchener to mop up the mess created by the top brass including Kitchener himself. Hamilton never looks happy to play a part in condemning the men and shows some sympathies towards them, but ultimately knows he must carry out his duty, no matter how onerous.

The standout member of the cast is Jack Thompson. Already a highly respected and experienced star of stage and screen (both big and small), Thompson is perfect as the beleaguered Major James. Handed a poisoned chalice and expected to provide nothing more than a token gesture, James frequently wins arguments, destroys hostile witnesses, and comes up with persistent points of law, procedure and Army protocol in his efforts to have the three men acquitted. James sees the trial for the sham it is, but never stops in his efforts to see justice prevail and the three men set free. His look of abject defeat at the end when the sentences have been passed down is borne of genuine sadness, but also sheer bloody frustration. He knows he's right, knows he's done enough to get them freed, but realises that all the time he's been working with both hands tied behind his back. Thompson is superb as the world-weary former solicitor thrown in way over his head, surprising everyone with the gusto of his defence. Most of the time, he's courteous, polite and mild-mannered, but woe betide anyone who ruffles his feathers too much! Those who prevaricate or lie feel like they've stepped on a rake when James verbally tears them apart.

Almost from the word go on the first day of the trial, Beresford draws the battle lines and establishes the class structure with a piece of cinematic simplicity. As the court convenes, the British (prosecution and judges) walk in and solemnly remove their British Army issue pith helmets, while Morant, Handcock, Witton and James remove their Aussie issue slouch hats. On the one side stand the stiff, proper, rigid Brits, looking down their noses; on the other stand the more relaxed, easy-going colonials who are expected to know their place. Beresford happily embraces the film's stage-bound roots as the three men are charged and the court proceedings begin, but at the earliest opportunity he opens the film up and takes the action out of the courtroom, the cell blocks and the offices of the high and mighty, and up onto the wide open South African veldt, giving us flashbacks to the events that led to the trial.

Witton may be shown as a naïve victim of circumstances, but Beresford never makes the mistake of trying to portray Morant and Handcock as anything other than guilty of shooting Boer prisoners. The film isn't about their innocence or guilt; it is about their actions and the moral ambiguity of normal men in abnormal circumstances being judged against the expectations of normal Edwardian society. Morant is a good, if slightly unconventional, soldier who follows orders even if he dislikes them, but is driven off the rails by the brutal murder of his commanding officer and good friend, Captain Hunt. It's Hunt who first tells Morant to carry out the shooting of Boer prisoners that have been brought in, but these are only ever verbal orders and therefore the High Command are able to disown and deny them later. As Morant, Handcock and Witton learn to their cost, it's okay to order bad things to be done just so long as you have the position and privilege to cover it up afterwards. Kitchener and his staff are just as culpable of atrocities and possible war crimes, but they have powerful friends who come to their aid as soon as a whiff of scandal or impropriety rears its head. Any friends the three men might have called upon have been quickly dispatched to India or other far-flung corners of the British Empire to stop them giving any evidence.

As far as British Army Command is concerned, the men's guilt can never be questioned, and their innocence can never be proven. This gives the opportunity for a trio of wonderful prosecution witnesses to be brought forward. First, Capt. Robertson (Rob Steele), who was in charge of the Bushveldt Carbineers until replaced by Morant. Uneasy in an ill-fitting brown pinstripe suit, Robertson quickly finds his evidence being shredded by Major Thomas and looks like a rabbit caught in the headlamps of a car he's voluntarily stepped in front of. His appearance in the court seems borne more out of annoyance at a perceived slight than any personal animosity against the three defendants.

His manner suggests he's there under orders and, in a small way perhaps, has a grudging respect for Morant, Handcock and their actions. Robertson is quickly followed by Sgt-Major Drummond (Ray Meagher) who clearly has a beef against both Morant and particularly Handcock.

Drummond portrays himself as a blameless paragon of virtue and exchanges insults with Handcock, but only Handcock is chided by the court and told that any more outbursts will land him in trouble (which, considering the murder charge against him, seems the least of his worries). The jewel in the crown is the third witness, Corporal Sharp (Chris Haywood), who might be one of the most inappropriately named characters in history. Every time he opens his mouth, the only evidence he gives is that he's the bluntest of tools who simply regurgitates the words

and testimony he's been trained to say. It's a wonderful little cameo from Haywood. We may smile at his lack of intelligence and ease of manipulation, but we also find ourselves shaking our head at the thought of such a biased and corrupt witness being taken so seriously.

With so much of the film being set in and around the courtroom and the cell block, it would have been easy for it to become bogged down with too much talk and too little action. Beresford is shrewd enough to liven things up with a Boer attack on the garrison where the trial is taking place. The Boers ride slowly towards the encamped soldiers outside the fort while one of their women 'distracts' a British guard who learns the hard way that smooching on duty is not necessarily a good idea as a bundle of dynamite blows his world and other attributes away. The British are taken so completely by surprise that Morant, Handcock and Witton are pressed into action by their guards to stop the Boers overrunning the garrison, something the three men grudgingly agree to do if only to "break the monotony" as Handcock quips afterwards. Major Thomas suggests that their actions should have some bearing on proceedings, that they should go some way to seeing the charges dismissed, but once again (and not totally unexpectedly) Col. Denny dismisses the point out of hand and insists it has no effect on the sympathies of the court.

The Boers, in reality little more than armed farmers, are portrayed as brave, tenacious and resourceful fighters. They aren't fighting for a cause or money, they're fighting for the very land they walk on. The British, on the other hand, are professional soldiers paid by the government with no stake in the outcome of the conflict, and at times it tells. The British are shown as slightly pompous and snobbish with a pervading sense of superiority. Beresford never strays into Brit-bashing for the sake of it, the way many felt Mel Gibson did in *Braveheart* and *The Patriot*. Instead, he shows the British as they probably were at a time when the Empire was at its zenith - rightly proud that a small rock in the North Sea rules over a quarter of the globe, but bearing the baggage and arrogance that comes with having forged an Empire of such magnitude. Beresford never kicks them for the sake of it, but nevertheless probably enjoyed the fact the British aren't shown in a particularly good light. The Boers are depicted more compassionately but are still shown to have zero sympathy with anyone taking sides with the British. They deal with them in brutal fashion. Morant has a Boer guide working for him, and in the flashbacks the guide is shown to be an enthusiastic and willing member of the firing squad. However, by the time the trial begins, he's fully aware of the precarious position he's in and agrees to appear for the prosecution in the hope that it will placate his fellow Boers. It doesn't.

Gunned down in the street, his body is left as warning to anyone else who may want to follow his lead. In the end, when all is said and done, when the proceedings reach their conclusion, we're left with the sight of Morant and Handcock walking towards their date with the firing squad hand in hand, something Woodward and Brown improvised on the spot with no prior knowledge that the real Morant and Handcock actually did precisely that. It's a beautifully played scene, with both Woodward and Brown accepting the inevitable but still unable to resist a final show of defiance as Woodward shouts: "Shoot straight you bastards! Don't make a mess of it." Sadly for Morant and Handcock, they don't.

The end credits briefly show what happened to the other main characters. If further proof is needed that the men truly were scapegoats of the empire (the title of Witton's book about the incident), it's the fact that after all the machinations and purported outrage at what they did, Witton ended up only serving three years in prison.

Although set in South Africa, the entire film was shot between March and June 1979 in and around the small town of Burra in South Australia. It's to cinematographer Donald McAlpine's credit that you never notice. His palette is made up of khaki, dusty brown and drab beige tones with the only splash of any other colour appearing in the offices of Lord Kitchener, and that only briefly. His camerawork for the final scenes is excellent, capturing the sun rising over the hills, silhouetting Morant and Handcock against the soft early morning light. McAlpine

had previously worked on *My Brilliant Career* and would go on to shoot *Moscow on the Hudson*, *Down and Out in Beverley Hills* and *Moulin Rouge* in a career that saw him almost continuously employed since 1969.

Breaker Morant was a financial and critical success, despite not being an easy film to categorise. It's not a straightforward war film as there's very little action, and probably its closest relative is Stanley Kubrick's *Paths of Glory* though this isn't as overtly anti-war. It virtually swept the 1980 Australian Academy of Cinema and Television Arts Awards, winning Best Film, Editing, Costume Design, Cinematography, Production Design, Sound and Best Director for Bruce Beresford. Meanwhile Jack Thompson and Bryan Brown won the Best Actor and Best Supporting Actor awards. Beresford, Stevens and Hardy also won for Best Screenplay and garnered the film's only Academy Award nomination, but lost out to *Ordinary People*. The only major international prize the film won was at the 1980 Cannes Film Festival, where Jack Thompson picked up a thoroughly deserved Best Supporting Actor award. Although Beresford went on to make *Tender Mercies*, *Crimes of the Heart*, *Mister Johnson* and *Driving Miss Daisy*, he claimed he'd always be best remembered for *Breaker Morant* and I don't think that's a bad thing. The film demands your attention, constantly poses questions and reveals new angles and fresh perspectives with each viewing. It was a story that needed to be told, and told properly. As Morant said: "Don't make a mess of it", and Beresford certainly didn't.

MANHUNTER

by Darren Linder

Manhunter was one of the first movies that I obsessed on as a teenager, which is fitting as it's a film about obsession. It also offered us our first glimpse on screen of the infamous character Hannibal Lecter, played very differently here than in *The Silence of the Lambs* several years later. The film concerns a retired FBI profiler, Will Graham (William Petersen), who is drawn back in to work on a disturbing case involving a serial killer who murders entire families and bases his slaughter on lunar cycles. In his hurried hunt to catch the killer before the next family is killed, the profiler consults a serial killer he'd helped to capture for advice and to get back into the mindset. The incarcerated prisoner is, of course, Hannibal Lecktor (note the spelling – '<u>Lecktor</u>' in this film, '<u>Lecter</u>' in the book and Jonathan Demme's *The Silence of the Lambs*).

Michael Mann released this dark masterpiece in 1986 after the success of his TV series *Miami Vice*. He had previously made the James Caan heist film *Thief* (1981) and the moody horror *The Keep* (1983). He was still a new director with a lot of buzz around him. Very stylized visual films with lengthy music cues had become popular at the time, in part because of his show *Miami Vice*. In his first two movies, he brilliantly used the German group Tangerine Dream for the soundtracks. For *Manhunter*, he branched out and used more current bands, like Shriekback, plus classic rock from Iron Butterfly, still managing to retain the pulsing and atmospheric soundscape.

Mann meticulously researched every detail for authenticity. He used actual former professional burglars as on-set consultants on *Thief* to make the technical scenes as genuine as possible. He recorded actual gunfire on location for the infamous shootout in *Heat* (1995) because he wanted realistic gunshots bouncing off the concrete buildings instead of pre-recorded sounds from audio libraries. It is commonly agreed that since Mann delves so deeply into research and detailed productions, he releases films at a slower rate than other directors.

Manhunter oozes great '80s aesthetics, from the color palette to the music. Note how frequently green is the dominant color on screen, representing sickness. The film is a mood piece which sustains the intensity for its entire two hours by wonderfully blending music, acting, editing and gorgeous cinematography by Dante Spinotti. It is deathly serious, with absolutely no comic relief or moments of levity to break up the unrelentingly dark subject matter. And nor should there be any. The only other film I can think of which stays so deep in this level of focused death-mood is David Fincher's *Se7en* (1995), and even that has a moment or two of normalcy and awkward humor. *Manhunter* gives absolutely no quarter, which may be why it didn't make much money at the box office. The behind-the-scenes machinations of the detective team working through the evidence and trying to prevent the next killing are fascinating to watch. And the marriage of music to certain images is unforgettable.

During a scene where Graham analyzes videotape evidence in a hotel room, Mann uses blocking to reinforce what is happening. Graham starts the scene sitting in front of the hotel TV with the camera placed behind it. What's interesting is that the director has the back of the TV block out 50% of the image. I don't think I've seen a director do this before. Then Graham remembers to check in with his wife, so he moves to the hotel bed, turning his back on the camera, and the camera moves to the side so there is nothing blocking our view of the white hotel room. Once he has checked in with her, he can focus on his work with no distractions or guilt. When he returns to the chair, the television now covers about two-thirds of the screen. The darkness of his work can now take up more of his life, just as the blackness of the TV is literally taking over more and more of the screen.

Mann tends to revisit certain themes in many of his films. He is particularly interested in the similarities between career criminals and the law enforcers who try to catch them. To be a good detective, you have to think like a criminal and know your enemy. His films suggest that both sides are so similar to each other that one could easily switch allegiances and be successful. Films like *Manhunter*,

Thief and *Heat* all deal with this dichotomy. *Manhunter* is about a profiler putting himself in the same mindset as the killer to help predict his actions and catch him. But the danger of delving too deep into the mind of a murderer is, of course, that the profiler might actually end up damaged. Mann dealt with this exact same storyline in an episode of *Miami Vice* called *Shadow in the Dark* from Season Three, with Don Johnson's Crockett as the Will Graham profiler character.

Mann has motifs that he repeats specifically in his crime pictures. If you examine the holy trifecta of perfect Mann films - *Thief, Manhunter* and *Heat* - you'll see similar scenes in each one. Characters making big decisions or having big discussions near bodies of water. Men obsessed with catching or killing another man. Shots of people in rooms with floor-to-ceiling windows, the ocean outside and a blue hue lighting everything. Characters repeating the line: "Time is luck." Amazing exchanges of dialogue and personal disclosures over coffee at a diner. The respective girlfriends or wives being pushed away to keep them out of danger, or neglected or abandoned because the job always comes first. He has violent cat-and-mouse denouements full of blood squibs and bullets, and loud music on the soundtrack. All three films have the famous shot of the main character aiming a gun directly at the camera. They all deal with honor among thieves, being a professional and living by a code. Similar to Sam Peckinpah's *The Wild Bunch*, most of Mann's films involve men out of time, whose usefulness and relevancy are quickly running out. As the lead character in *The Wild Bunch* says: "We've gotta start thinking beyond our guns. Those days are closing fast."

Thomas Harris wrote 'Black Sunday' in 1975, and it was made into a movie of the same name in 1977. Being a fan of his first book, I found his second, *Red Dragon*, soon after it was published in 1981 and loved it. When I started seeing commercials for a screen version done by the great Michael Mann, I was beyond excited. I had been staying up to watch *Miami Vice* on network television, and later *Crime Story*. I rented his heist film *Thief* countless times on VHS. I was even one of the dozen or so people who saw the film *Band of the Hand* in theaters in 1986, which played like an R-rated feature length episode of *Miami Vice* and was produced by Mann's production company. I bought several copies of 'Red Dragon' and read it numerous times before seeing the movie. I had both a one-sheet poster and a 3-D cardboard promotional display that I purchased

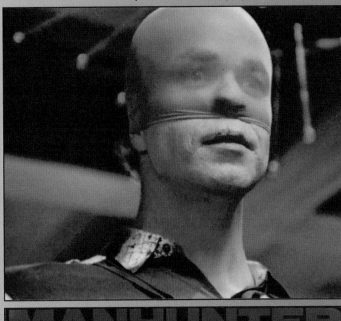

from our local videotape rental store. I bought the soundtrack on vinyl and listened to the three songs from Shriekback over and over on headphones. And, of course, I've upgraded over the years, owning it on VHS, DVD and Blu-Ray. The limited edition DVD release of the director's cut is interesting as a curiosity, but I honestly prefer the theatrical version.

When *Manhunter* came out in theaters in 1986, I had to make a plan to see it. I wasn't old enough to go see an R-rated film by myself, so I had to convince my parents to take me. To make things more difficult, this film certainly was not going to be a blockbuster and would likely disappear from theaters quickly. Even more challenging was that my family was on a vacation in Hawaii for the opening night of the film. But my parents were supportive of me and my love of movies, so they helped me find a theater in Hawaii where *Manhunter* was screening. If you weren't 17 you had to get your parents to buy tickets and attend with you. We took time off from snorkeling and luau vacation activities to set me up to see *Manhunter* in theaters. They honestly had no interest in seeing a dark drama about catching a serial killer, so they made sure I got in then, I assume, went for coffee and hung out for two hours while I was transported into another world. Even better, it was during the daytime and nobody else was in the theater because they were all on the beach. This was one of the most fun and transformative theater experiences of my life. Thanks, Mom and Dad.

I've always felt that Petersen did a phenomenal job of carrying this film, conveying the character's previous trauma and overall focus and intensity. The scene in the grocery store where he finally tells his son what exactly happened that sent him to the hospital is a master class in acting. Handsome and capable, I will forever think of the man as Will Graham. He has a lot of dialogue and is in almost every scene, often sitting alone in a room talking to himself while analyzing evidence. Some actors couldn't pull this off, but he is great. Between the two-punch run of *To Live and Die in L.A.* (1985) and *Manhunter* (1986), Petersen should have become a much more well-known actor than he is. He did go on to portray a very similar character for over a decade in

It's just you and me now, sport...

MANHUNTER

DE LAURENTIIS ENTERTAINMENT GROUP Presents
A RICHARD ROTH Production A MICHAEL MANN Film "MANHUNTER" WILLIAM PETERSEN KIM GREIST JOAN ALLEN BRIAN COX
DENNIS FARINA STEPHEN LANG and TOM NOONAN Edited by DOV HOENIG Production Designer MEL BOURNE Director of Photography DANTE SPINOTTI
Executive Producer BERNARD WILLIAMS Based on the Book "Red Dragon" by THOMAS HARRIS Screenplay by MICHAEL MANN Produced by RICHARD ROTH Directed by MICHAEL MANN

the successful series *CSI* (*Crime Scene Investigation*).

Another assertion I've had for a very long time now is that Brian Cox gives a better and more believable performance than Anthony Hopkins as Hannibal Lecktor. Much like Hopkins in the 1991 film *The Silence of the Lambs*, Cox is only in *Manhunter* for three scenes and has very little screen time. He has approximately 9 minutes in total, while Hopkins had approximately 24 minutes altogether in the later movie. But both appearances completely dominate their respective films, making ripples and echoes through scenes they aren't even in. The resonating power of their evil permeates the two pictures like a malignant cancer.

No offense to Hopkins or director Demme, but the Lecter role in *The Silence of the Lambs* is very showy and feels like a performance. It's very exaggerated and seems as if a screenwriter had fun creating the scenes but perhaps went too far. Watching Hopkins, we are watching a Hollywood actor reading lines and hoping to get an award. Watching Cox feels more like we are seeing a documentary with actual footage of a serial killer. If the Hopkins version is aggrandized narcissism, then the Cox version is more realistic and restrained antisocial behavior. I believe that most actual murderers are more like the latter than the former. The Brian Cox version is more like an everyman, able to blend in with society. Upon dozens of viewings of both films, the Hopkins read on the character can feel like Kabuki Theater. I can appreciate the theatrics of it all, but I am much more creeped out and rattled by Cox's sinister portrayal.

The integral scene where we first meet Lecktor is a high point of the film. We see a non-remarkable man imprisoned but still causing much anxiety to the profiler through the stark white prison cell bars. It's clear how traumatizing it is for Graham to even be in the same room as Lecktor.

Lecktor hurt him when he was captured and Graham was in the hospital recovering from physical injury and mental injury. It's a simple scene on paper, with one man locked in a cell and another man outside the cell talking to each other. They are both trying to get information from the other without revealing anything. The music goes against expectation by being the most relaxing and peaceful track in the film. Mann used German electronic artist Klaus Schulze's song *Freeze* for this stressful mutual interrogation scene. The song always makes me think of wooden wind chimes on a beach. It's mesmerizing and perfect.

Mann perfectly centers the men's faces inside the visual boxes that the bars create, showing that in different ways, both are trapped in their worlds. Graham is typically framed by the bars very close to the sides of his head, as if he is being squeezed in a vice grip. His past is closing in on him. Lecktor's face is often bisected by the cell bars, showing his ability to move outside restrictions and expectations. We can't always see the true person as he is partially obscured. Everything in the cell is white, from the bars to the walls. Also notice there are no shadows in this cell, as if the light has been sucked out of the room by the evil inside.

This is an unwanted reunion, and also a confrontation or challenge. Above all else it is a huge gamble. It is akin to the famous scene in Mann's crime epic *Heat* where the

Al Pacino and Robert De Niro characters meet for coffee in a diner and size each other up. But in this case, Lecktor gets under Graham's skin and causes him to have a panic attack. Graham has to run outside of the sterile, white, concrete psychiatric prison and get closer to nature to ground himself. He stares at the green grass, which goes from blurry to focused as he gathers himself.

After about an hour of following Will Graham on this police procedural, we finally meet the killer, Francis Dollarhyde, aka 'The Tooth Fairy.' Played by the great Tom Noonan, he perfectly embodies a severely abused and awkward child now grown up. The book deals more with his childhood abuse and his having a cleft palate which, as a kid, resulted in others mocking and tormenting him. If you watch his performance, it is full of great little tics like him bringing his hand up to cover his mouth when someone enters the room. His physical insecurities and feeling like the outsider are masterfully shown. He has a childlike manner when relating with other people, naïve and awkward. Later in the film, after sleeping with his new girlfriend, he pulls her hand up to his own mouth to cover it as he sobs. It's a surprising and unique performance that gets better each time I watch it.

Dollarhyde meets Reba, a blind coworker who obviously is not affected by his odd appearance, his cleft palate, or being a social outcast. Joan Allen plays Reba magnificently,

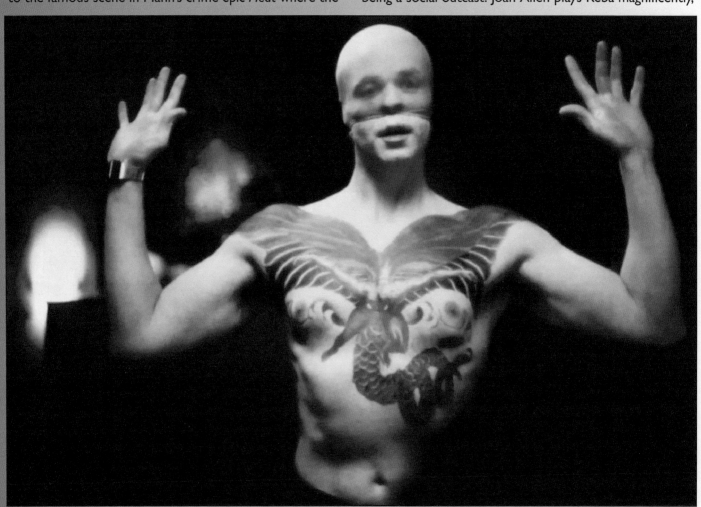

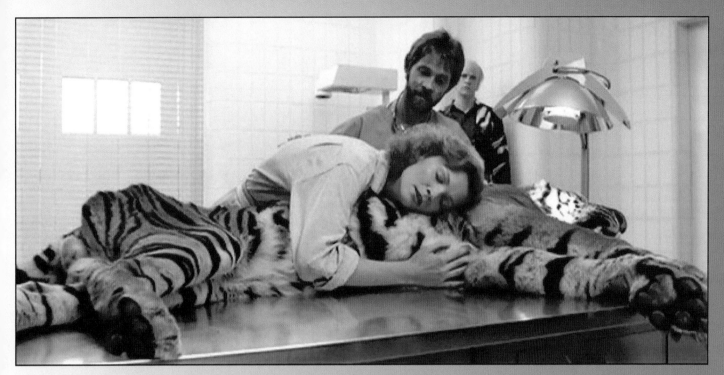

in only her second film role. Dollarhyde connecting with a blind woman is very interesting, not only because she wouldn't see his physical imperfections, but also because everything about his character is to do with 'seeing'. When he shows kidnapped reporter Lounds slides of the past and future victims, he repeats the question, "Do you see?" like a mantra. He works in a photographic processing plant. He takes photos or video of him murdering the families and then watches them later. He views home movies of the victims just like the FBI profiler does. He punches a mirror in slow motion, and then puts the broken pieces on the eyes of the victims so he can see himself reflected. Graham says: "Because everything with you is seeing, isn't it? Your primary sensory intake that makes your dream live is seeing... reflections... mirrors... images..." Him falling for Reba makes sense on so many psychological levels. She can never see what he has done, or see the real him.

The scene that I want to highlight, and that haunts me, involves a tiger.

Reba warms to Dollarhyde and he decides to take her on a surprise car ride somewhere. We fear that he is targeting her due to her blindness and that she is in peril of being his next victim. Instead, we are treated to one of the most powerful scenes in all of cinema.

Dollarhyde brings Reba to the office of a veterinarian he knows, and the doctor explains that they have an adult tiger sedated awaiting dental surgery. In one of the most perfectly chosen matches of music to imagery, Shriekback's exquisite and moody song *Coelacanth* pulses on the soundtrack. Reba runs her hands through the tiger's thick fur while in no danger, even pulling open the tiger's mouth to touch its huge fangs. She feels the tiger's hot breath on her wrist. The doctor guides her hand to the tiger's heart and she puts her ear onto its body, wrapping her

arms around the tiger and hugging it. She hears and feels this huge animal's heartbeat like only a handful of people ever have. (Dollarhyde later puts his head on Reba's chest as she sleeps, listening to her heartbeat in a reflection of this scene).

This sedated tiger scene is emotional and touching in a way we do not expect in a film about hunting a serial killer. Reba has a spiritual and sublime experience with this tiger and cries tears of joy, while Dollarhyde stands in the corner watching them, having his own rapturous experience away from the others. The psychopath gives another human being this unique gift of tactile connection with an animal, yet he remains alone and disconnected. He does not bond with her during this moment. The idea of someone without sight getting to experience this with heightened touch and hearing is incredibly powerful. She is 'seeing' this animal with her hands and ears, and Dollarhyde gave her this moment. The scene is obviously symbolic of getting very close to a creature that could easily kill you, as she is doing with Dollarhyde himself. This scene is only two minutes long, but I could put it on repeat and watch it for an hour straight. It's one of my favorite scenes in any film, and it still gives me chills when I watch it.

Manhunter remains one of my favorite movies. It sets the bar for police procedural films in which a profiler hunts for a serial killer. It has a mesmerizing soundtrack, a skilled director, great actors, the best screen incarnation of Hannibal Lecktor and is my favorite film of the franchise. Every time I watch it, I feel like a teenager on the Hawaiian beach listening to wooden wind chimes while looking out at the ocean thinking about my life.

The Ninth Configuration

A Unique Film Experience

by David Flack

Like everyone who contributes to this magazine, I love film. I try to watch a film a day - new, old, classics, not so classic, favourites that I've seen over and over, anything, it doesn't matter. Once in a while, I come across a movie which really strikes a chord, affecting me and enhancing my film enjoyment. One such case is William Peter Blatty's *The Ninth Configuration*, a unique, wonderful movie which defies description. When I first saw it, it went straight onto my list of personal top 30 all-time favourites. I returned to it to prepare for this article, and found myself laughing and crying more than I did even on my first viewing. I have seen it now ten times, and on each occasion I picked up something fresh and new.

The plot is briefly this: Vincent Kane (Stacy Keach), formerly a marine, now a psychiatrist, takes over at an army asylum situated in a remote castle. He must determine which patients are really ill and which are faking mental illness. He has a unique way of doing this and comes into conflict over religious beliefs with Captain Billy Cutshaw (Scott Wilson), an ex-astronaut who went berserk and refused to go to the moon. As things develop, it turns out the asylum's new chief has very dark secrets of his own.

That is all I will reveal. The less you know, the more you will enjoy the film's twists and turns. If you've seen it, you'll know what I mean. If you haven't, you are in for a treat and I truly envy you. Just let the film wash over you and do its magic.

Based on Blatty's **1966** novel 'Twinkle, Twinkle, "Killer" Kane' (the film's American release title), the screen version marked Blatty's directorial debut. He'd go on to

direct the very good *Exorcist 3: Legion* (1990), which was also based on one of his novels and for which he wrote the adapted screenplay. I genuinely wish he had directed more. *The Ninth Configuration* was made on a $4,000,000 budget and filmed in Hungary, though it is set in America. I would imagine a big chunk of that budget went on paying the cast, and what a cast it is!

The line-up features Stacy Keach, Scott Wilson, Ed Flanders, Jason Miller, Neville Brand, Robert Loggia, Joe Spinell, George DiCenzo, Alejandro Rey, Moses Gunn, Tom Atkins, Steve Sandor and Richard Lynch, all of whom are excellent or very memorable in their roles. The trio of Keach, Wilson and Miller are three of my favourite actors in general, the first two for the bulk of their career work and Miller, of course, for his brilliant portrayal of Father Karras in *The Exorcist* (1973) amongst others. (Speaking of *The Exorcist*, *that* too was, of course, based on Blatty's novel and again he wrote the screenplay for the screen adaptation, though on that occasion the directing duties fell to William Friedkin). In addition, Blatty appears uncredited in *The Ninth Configuration* in a hilarious cameo as Lieutenant Fromme.

There are five versions of *The Ninth Configuration* ranging from 99 to 140 minutes. Blatty only approved the 118-minute version, which is the one I own and watched for this article. It has a previously unseen scene before the credits featuring the song *San Antone* by Denny Brooks

(which also plays over the opening credits of the 1977 film *Rolling Thunder*). As the song plays, we see Cutshaw looking forlorn and staring out the castle's windows. It seems a fairly innocuous shot, and it's only when you've seen the film several times that it becomes significant. This scene is omitted from the four other versions; instead, they start with a foreboding dream/flashback sequence during which the credits play over a scene showing a moon rocket launch pad and a menacing, outsize moon.

'Twinkle, Twinkle, "Killer" Kane' was the second of Blatty's 'Faith' trilogy (the others being 'The Exorcist' and 'Legion'). There seems to be some confusion and a bit of a myth about the connection between *The Ninth Configuration* and *The Exorcist*. There is a character in *The Exorcist* who attends Regan's mother's house party. He is an astronaut, and the demonically possessed Regan says to him: "You're going to die up there." It is widely assumed that this character is Captain Cutshaw, but it is not necessarily so. The character in the book and the film is not named, and the end credits refer to him merely as 'astronaut'.

I am about to wax lyrical about the good points of *The Ninth Configuration*, but before I do there are a few criticisms that should be addressed. For one thing, many critics have pointed out that the asylum inmates are grossly exaggerated and unreal. To be honest, it's a fair point. But if you accept the way they are presented as an example of 'artistic licence', it makes the film immensely entertaining. The film does at times look and feel like a play, but the acting is so good you barely notice. Towards the climax, it concentrates mainly on the characters Kane, Cutshaw

Don't blink for a second because nothing is what it seems.

WILLIAM PETER BLATTY'S **TWINKLE, TWINKLE, "KILLER" KANE**

...it may change your life.

A WILLIAM PETER BLATTY FILM "TWINKLE, TWINKLE, "KILLER" KANE"
Starring STACY KEACH · SCOTT WILSON · JASON MILLER · ED FLANDERS · NEVILLE BRAND
GEORGE DICENZO · MOSES GUNN · ROBERT LOGGIA
Written, Produced and Directed by WILLIAM PETER BLATTY · Music by BARRY DeVORZON
Director of photography GERRY FISHER, B.S.C.
Released by UNITED FILM DISTRIBUTION CO.

and Fell; the other inmates, whom the story has taken pains to endear to the audience, are thrust mostly to the background and their fates are left unknown. However, the emotional power and impact of the film is huge, so I'm perfectly happy to overlook these minor shortcomings.

It is a film of two halves. The first half is primarily a wacky, insane comedy, broader than *One Flew Over the Cuckoo's Nest* (1975), hilarious like *Hellzapoppin'* (1941) or any Marx Brothers comedy, only wilder. There are so many movie references and so much quotable dialogue, it really is a film buff's delight. It comes at you so fast that at first you are thrown off balance and think: "What the hell am I watching here?" There is so much going on visually and particularly audibly that it's impossible to catch it all on one viewing. In fact, I still find new things on each viewing and never get bored revisiting the movie.

The opening parade scene sets the tone; the dialogue is brilliant and incredibly funny. Among the standout scenes are one which comically dissects the meaning of Shakespeare's 'Hamlet', Cutshaw's "Don't order the swordfish" monologue, Major Groper's love letters prank, and Jason Miller's character Frank Reno attempting to put on a production of 'Hamlet' entirely with a cast of dogs! The audition scenes and the antics of the canine cast are funny. The scene where Reno and his casting director (played by Joe Spinell) discuss the casting is a highlight. In fact, all the actors excel and show a great flair for comedy, particularly Wilson, Ed Flanders and Miller.

The second half becomes much darker and is a psychological drama, a clash of beliefs story. The humour is still there, but the dialogue becomes emotional, powerful and thought-provoking.

There are two excellently acted scenes between Kane and Cutshaw. The one where they debate "If God exists, why is there so much cruelty in the world?" is brilliant. This is due to Keach and Wilson's acting, and Blatty's writing. The moment when Cutshaw challenges Kane to give one example of man's goodness is heart-breaking. Kane gives him two examples which Cutshaw explains away, then Kane falters searching for a third and you can see the devastation and despair in Cutshaw's face. He desperately wants to be persuaded that he should believe there is goodness in the world. The same can be said of the later scene in which Kane asks Cutshaw: "Why wouldn't you go to the moon?" Again, Wilson conveys so much in his face, eyes and voice as he recounts why. Both scenes reduce me to tears, and Wilson's performance is one of the best I have ever seen. That he was not even nominated for an Oscar is a travesty. Nowadays better known for his role as Herschel in the TV series *The Walking Dead*, Wilson had much more than that to his career. He gave great performances in films like *In Cold Blood* (1967), *The Grissom Gang* (1971), *The New Centurions* (1972), *Malone* (1987) and *Hostiles* (2017) to name a few. He was an underrated, neglected actor.

Keach has been criticised in some circles for giving a flat, robot-like performance, and he certainly plays second fiddle to Wilson's towering performance. But Vincent Kane is a man who has seen much violence and horror and is battling his remorse. He truly believes he has been given a chance of redemption by helping these men. Keach's performance is pitch perfect. He is incredible and pulls off a difficult role remarkably well. One scene, where he sits alone and the camera has him in long shot - slowly closing in so that you can see he is crying silently - is unbelievably moving. We see him battling his personal demons inside, a feeling I know well in my own life.

The Ninth Configuration is an effective tour-de-force of acting, with only one scene containing any real action. And what a jolting, memorable scene it is - a quick, violent, brutal, stunningly staged bar fight that is realistically claustrophobic.

The film may at times be bewildering in its change of tone, but all is revealed in an engaging manner as the twists and turns lead to a clever denouement. Some critics have issues with the ending, but I think it is excellent, if somewhat abrupt, and touchingly uplifting.

I have mentioned Keach and Wilson's excellent portrayals, but I must say the whole cast is superb. Special

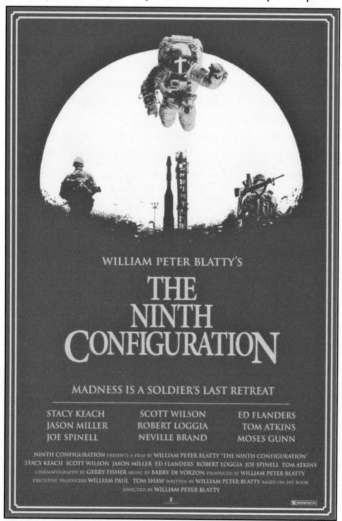

mention should be made of Ed Flanders as Colonel Fell who is magnificent in a complex role. His performance seems to be forgotten, but it is so important and significant to the film. Kudos to Miller too as Frank Reno and his insane quest to bring the canine version of Shakespeare's 'Hamlet' to life, and Neville Brand who is very good in one of his last roles as Major Gruber. Although much maligned and abused, he proves himself at the climax.

Finally, a word on William Peter Blatty who, to my mind, was a genius. A witty, deeply religious and intelligent man, he started out writing screenplays for comedies including *A Shot in the Dark* (1964), the second - and one of the best - of Blake Edwards' *Pink Panther* films. However, he is best known for his novels and scripts for the likes of *The Exorcist*, *Exorcist 3* and *The Ninth Configuration*, directing the latter two. It is such a shame he did not direct more, as these are powerful, intelligent and thoughtful films.

Love it or hate it, once you've seen *The Ninth Configuration*, you won't forget it. It is a unique experience and, for me personally, a very special near-masterpiece.

(I would like to dedicate this article to Joseph Parra, a man I never met in person but who was a good Facebook friend. I know he was loved by many other film fans, theatre actors, writers and readers of this magazine and its sister mag, 'Cinema of the '70's'. You are much missed, Joseph, my friend - R.I.P.)

WOODY ALLEN IN THE '80s
America's Greatest Clown Continues to Grow Up

By Dr. Andrew C. Webber

Woody Allen had already lost a great many admirers at the tail end of the '70s when he made the badly received *Interiors* (his first "serious" film). The caustic *Stardust Memories*, his first film of the '80s, appeared next and seemed to belittle his fans and suggested he found the whole movie-making thing soul-destroying and soulless. It was enough to alienate some fans even further.

However, to say that he more than made up for this in the rest of the decade is a major understatement - yes, there were occasional misfires (*September* is one I have little desrire to revisit), but this was a decade in which he made at least two of his greatest films (*Zelig* and *Crimes and Misdemeanors*). He also knocked out the much-loved (at the time) *The Purple Rose of Cairo*, *Hannah and Her Sisters* and *Radio Days*. Both *Broadway Danny Rose* and *A Midsummer Night's Sex Comedy* rightfully have their admirers too (or at least they used to, before... well, you know).

Yes, it was in the '80s that Allen really found his mojo - in spite of what may or may not have been going on at home.

During the decade he continued to work with muse and partner Mia Farrow (who, lest we forget, was always outstanding in his movies) but he also managed to work with some of the other greatest actors of his day: Michael Caine, Gene Hackman, Charlotte Rampling, Gena Rowlands, John Houseman, Dianne Wiest, Carrie Fisher, Barbara Hershey, Max von Sydow, Anjelica Huston, Martin Landau, Alan Alda, Claire Bloom, Alec Baldwin, Judy Davis, William Hurt, Cybill Shepherd, Mary Steenburgen, Julie Haggerty, Sandy

Woody Allen
Charlotte Rampling
Jessica Harper
Marie-Christine Barrault
Tony Roberts

Stardust Memories

A Jack Rollins-Charles H. Joffe Production "Stardust Memories"
Producer Robert Greenhut Written and Directed by Woody Allen Executive Producers Jack Rollins-Charles H. Joffe
Director of Photography Gordon Willis Production Designer Mel Bourne United Artists A Transamerica Company

A MIDSUMMER NIGHT'S SEX COMEDY

Woody ALLEN   Mia FARROW
Jose FERRER   Mary STEENBURGEN
Julie HAGERTY   Tony ROBERTS

Denny, Ian Holm and Jose Ferrer. A list so impressive you have to read it twice. Did his small, low-budget New York-set comedy dramas, where everyone 'worked to scale' to keep costs down, really manage to attract so much talent?

At the time, of course, Allen was (ironically) respected as a first class director (and writer) of women and was also still casting himself in central roles where, as ever, he was brilliant (those who think Allen has little range should compare him in *Zelig, Broadway Danny Rose, Hannah and Her Sisters* and *Crimes and Misdemeanors* - four films in which he delivers superb performances, creating memorable characters who run through the range of emotions from tragic to hilarious). With the benefit of hindsight, it's obvious that he was both a key player in eliciting magnificent work from actresses (both old and young)

in an era where women's roles were often marginal *and* keeping his films funny enough to appeal to his '70s followers while allowing the themes and topics to grow darker as the years went by, ensuring he didn't just become a parody of himself. It's also worth noting that whilst Allen is most definitely one of America's most prolific *auteurs*, he is also one who clearly understands that the best films are collaborations. And he collaborated with not only the

finest actors of his (or any other generation) but also ensured that behind the scenes he was always in good company.

His '80s films continued to be shot in colour or black and white (or both in the case of *The Purple Rose of Cairo*) and his relationship with *Godfather* cinematographer Gordon Willis was central in the early part

of the decade. By its end, though, he was also working with Carlo Di Palma (with whom he shot his '90s masterpiece *Husbands and Wives* - his genius didn't expire in the '80s, folks) and Ingmar Bergman's legendary cameraman Sven Nykvist, who had won a justly-deserved Academy Award for *Cries and Whispers* (1972) as well as working with Bob Rafelson on his highly sexed *The Postman Always Rings Twice* re-make (1981), Bob Fosse on his little-seen *Star 80* (1983), Norman Jewison on *Agnes of God* (1985) and Phil Kaufman on *The Unbearable Lightness of Being* (1988).

Susan E. Morse continued to edit Allen's films (she'd worked with him on *Manhattan* but also found time to slot in the dated Dudley Moore comedy *Arthur* in 1980); production design was often done by Santo Loquasto, and the movies were all produced by Robert Greenhut who continued to work with Allen up until his musical (yup, you heard that

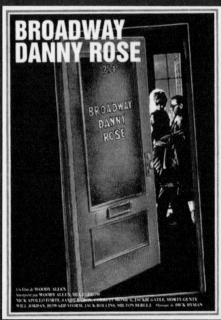

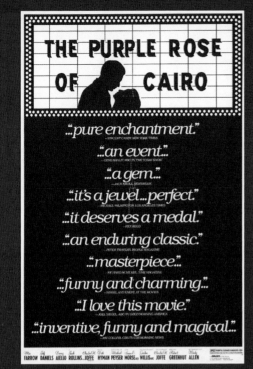

THE PURPLE ROSE OF CAIRO

"...*pure enchantment*."
—VINCENT CANBY, NEW YORK TIMES

"...*an event*..."
—GENE SHALIT, NBC-TV, THE TODAY SHOW

"...*a gem*..."
—JACK KROLL, NEWSWEEK

"...*it's a jewel...perfect*."
—MICHAEL WILMINGTON, LOS ANGELES TIMES

"...*it deserves a medal*."
—REX REED

"...*an enduring classic*."
—PETER TRAVERS, PEOPLE MAGAZINE

"...*masterpiece*..."
—RICHARD SCHICKEL, TIME MAGAZINE

"...*funny and charming*..."
—SISKEL AND EBERT, AT THE MOVIES

"...*I love this movie*."
—JOEL SIEGEL, ABC-TV, GOOD MORNING AMERICA

"...*inventive, funny and magical*..."
—PAT COLLINS, CBS-TV, CBS MORNING NEWS

HANNAH AND HER SISTERS

WOODY ALLEN   MICHAEL CAINE
MIA FARROW   CARRIE FISHER
BARBARA HERSHEY   LLOYD NOLAN
MAUREEN O'SULLIVAN   DANIEL STERN
MAX VON SYDOW   DIANNE WIEST

JACK ROLLINS AND CHARLES H. JOFFE ... SUSAN E. MORSE ... CARLO DI PALMA
JACK ROLLINS AND CHARLES H. JOFFE ... ROBERT GREENHUT   WOODY ALLEN

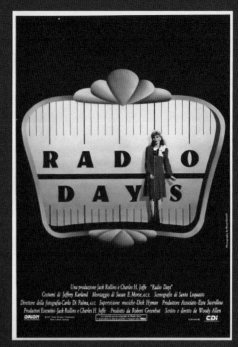

Una produzione Jack Rollins e Charles H. Joffe "Radio Days"

right) *Everyone Says I Love You* (1996). The music in his films, as ever, was a specially selected compendium of Allen's favourite jazz records. The opening credits remained, as ever, glorious white on black with the cast being given more-or-less equal billing. Every time the lights went down at one of Allen's new films, you knew what you were going to get yet, at the same time, it was always going to be a bit different too (rather like the sea).

And the awards and nominations kept coming. Actors who worked with Allen probably did their best work (maybe because he just left them alone to get on with it). Caine, Wiest and Allen himself all won Oscars for *Hannah* in '86 - his *annus mirabilis*, though his films were also nominated for Oscars almost every other year, often losing out to vastly inferior fare. *Zelig* was nominated for cinematography and costumes (but lost in both categories to Bergman's *Fanny and Alexander*); *Broadway Danny Rose* earned a nomination for best director (but Milos Forman won for *Amadeus*) and screenplay (with Robert Benton triumphing for *Places in the Heart*); *The Purple Rose of Cairo* was up for best script (*Witness* won); *Radio Days* for best script (*Moonstruck* won) and art direction (with *The Last Emperor* walking off with top prize); *Crimes and Misdemeanors* (in a year dominated by *Driving Miss Daisy*, of all things) was in the running for best director, screenplay and supporting actor (Martin Landau, who lost to Denzel Washington for *Glory*). I could go on, but it's enough to say that to date Allen has received a total of 16 Academy Award nominations for best screenwriter, an all-time record, apparently.

Whether he won or not, the point is that Allen's films were certainly acknowledged as significant works (at a time when the Oscars were a fairly good quality kite mark) and he was much loved by the Academy, even though he had failed to turn up to collect those illustrious statues in the '70s because he was playing jazz with his band in New York - a story which gains him much kudos in an era where actors and directors are almost contractually obligated to gurn their way through whatever promotional activity might add a few bucks to the market share of their latest release. Off screen, in the '80s - when, presumably his personal life was going off the rails - Allen remained private and guarded, and for that we should be grateful.

So, apart from his fantastic collaborators, superb screenplays and stunning performances, what else do Allen's '80s movies have to offer?

55

Essentially taken as a whole, the films continue to explore his great themes (a narrow track, well-furrowed): love and its opposite; Jewishness and the outsider; a love/love relationship with New York, cinema, theatre and jazz; lost opportunities; faith and doubt; childhood and growing older; and, in *Zelig,* which might be Allen's only overtly political film, America and the need to fit in at all costs. Allen remains one of Hollywood's greatest explorers of the role sex plays in relationships and he also has much to say about what we now describe as toxic masculinity. He's also interested in the intellect and what it means to be cultured in an uncivilized world (all of these explored in the unsung *Another Woman* - which is ripe for rediscovery if anyone ever returns to his oeuvre).

And considering that at his peak, Allen was one of cinema's greatest

clowns - up there with idols like Chaplin, the Marx brothers and Keaton - it comes as no surprise that so many of his movies often investigate the fine line there is in life between comedy and tragedy. They are filled with a wistful longing - it's those melancholy moments in films like *Zelig, Hannah and Her Sisters* and *Crimes and Misdemeanors* which really leave their mark. Those moments when we see behind the mask and gaze into the abyss - like Allen himself does at the end of *Crimes.*

As we all know, time has not been kind to Allen and his history has been significantly re-written over the last 30 years (whilst he has continued to make outstanding films like *Celebrity, Sweet and Lowdown* and *Blue Jasmine).* In spite of everything, he's carried on making movies into his eighties,

even if they have been increasingly hard to see (did *Rifkin's Festival* ever get released anywhere?) When I last checked on IMDB, there was even news of a new Woody Allen fall project (his 57th film as director, should it ever get made), an untitled return to Paris. Unsurprisingly, no news of cast is available at the time of writing this.

One wonders whether the damage done to Allen's reputation by aspects of his (previously) private life will outlive his films or vice versa? It's hard to say.

All I know is that a world without a new film by him each year already feels like a smaller one. When he's gone, it will feel even tinier.

He (and his complete opposite Clint Eastwood, whose own ideas about masculinity couldn't be more at odds with Allen's if they tried) have shaped my cinema going for over 50 years.

And we won't see their ilk again - whether we like it or not.

LEWIS COLLINS

WHO DARES ALMOST WINS

by Ian Taylor

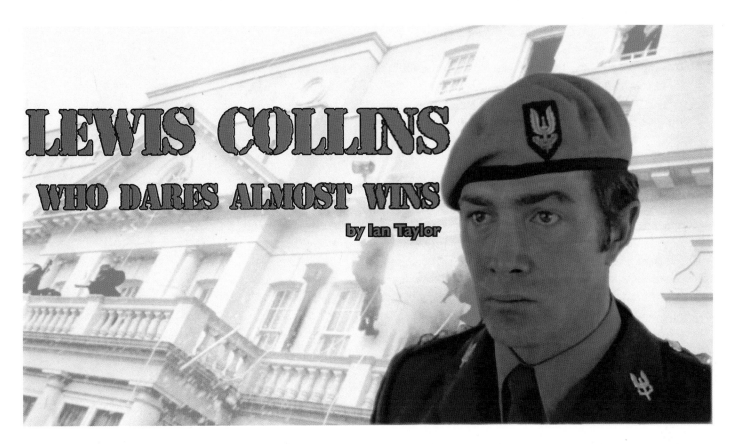

To understand the iconic status of macho yet mischievously mirthful action star Lewis Collins, one really needs to be British. That's not to say the late actor (taken tragically by cancer in 2013 at the age of 67) can't be enjoyed globally. He absolutely can. It's just that British kids of the mid-to-late '70s and through the '80s grew up with the fella. He should've been bigger, more famous, more successful - he came close - but, in the end, Lewis Collins remains a home-grown hero known elsewhere due to the vehicles he appeared *in* rather than *his* presence in them. It speaks volumes that the Official Lewis Collins Fan Site on the internet boasts over 300,000 British members whilst the nearest other nations (Germany and America respectively) can only manage just over 30,000 apiece. Nevertheless, the camera loved Collins, a man with looks, moves and charisma. After great success on UK television, particularly as one half of the crack action team *The Professionals*, the actor took the lead in the 1982 British movie *Who Dares Wins*.

Ill-informed observers will rubbish Collins, calling his performances pouty or sulky, daring to suggest he had less depth than his *The Professionals* co-star Martin Shaw. They are simply wrong. Collins was a truly artistic renaissance man; something missed no doubt due to him being as much an action man off screen as on, and the fact he spent his youth attending a very rough school where no-one offered books or plays to read because "we'd just throw them back." Nevertheless, Collins excelled in the creative elements of life as much as the rough and tumble, packing an incredible amount in pre-fame.

He was a drummer with his dad's band The Savoy Swingers at 13, moving onto around a half-dozen other bands, performing at Liverpool's legendary Cavern Club, even supporting The Beatles. Someone even suggested that he should apply to be their drummer when Pete Best left. He joined The Mojos, a well-known Mersey Beat group who enjoyed chart success and earned a record contract. This led to young Lewis having a Knightsbridge bachelor pad and being chauffeured around in a Rolls-Royce. But the music industry is fickle, and by 1966, the band had split, their manager was in jail and Collins was £2000 in debt.

Collins was also an apprentice hairdresser at Liverpool's prestigious André Bernard's, along with Peter Michael McCartney (aka Mike McGear), founder of novelty band The Scaffold (Lily the Pink) and brother of Paul McCartney. Collins found himself helping McGear plan ideas for The Scaffold, 'doing' singer Helen Shapiro's hair, appearing as a stooge to Ringo Starr in a television report and having Macca play him 'Love Me Do' before anyone else outside the Fab Four's team had heard it!

Collins was also a roadie, dishwasher, deliveryman, chauffeur, salesman, window-cleaner, waiter, Savile Row tailor's assistant and a lorry driver.

He joined LAMDA on a 3-year course in 1968, and despite his lack of literary/artistic knowledge, performed Shakespeare, made his professional stage debut in Strindberg's *Dance of Death* and had a successful stint at Glasgow's Citizen's Theatre, spending days off teaching drama to deaf children. He later taught drama to kids on a reservation in British Columbia and adults in Vancouver, Seattle and San Francisco.

Returning to the UK, he made his West End debut in 1973 and television debut in cop drama *Z-Cars* in 1974.

Collins also studiously indulged in judo and rifle shooting competitions. If it isn't dawning on anyone by now that the actor was anything but lacking in range and depth, then it should be!

Much later, Collins was asked about his action man status. He self-deprecatingly pointed out he was first known for comedy in Britain. Very true, thanks to his work in 1976, starting with a non-speaking bit part in the successful sex comedy *Confessions of a Driving Instructor* before landing one of the three principal roles in the romantic sitcom *The Cuckoo Waltz*. This made Collins a familiar face in the UK, and he stuck with the show for three series before looking to expand his range.

A pivotal moment came when he was cast in the role of bad guy Kilner in an episode of Brian Clemens' *New Avengers*. Prophetically, Collins played opposite Martin Shaw as the lead villain, and they didn't particularly get on. A year later, when Clemens had to recast the role of Bodie to play opposite Shaw's Doyle in *The Professionals*, the showrunner was certain that Shaw and Collins' abrasive relationship would be perfect. This resulted in a four-

year contract and an award-winning double act in a show that was required viewing in the UK, featuring car chases, punch-ups, gunfights, womanising and testosterone fuelled banter. Lewis Collins the action hero was born.

The show lasted for the four contracted years, although episodes were broadcast over 7 years between 1977 and 1983. Filming ceased in May 1981, leaving Collins looking for work, especially on the big screen.

As fate would have it, a seemingly perfect project was there for the taking. English producer Euan Lloyd (*Shalako*, *The Wild Geese*, *The Sea Wolves*) had been inspired to create a new movie by events surrounding the 1980 siege of the Iranian Embassy in London and the subsequent storming of the building by the Special Air Service (SAS). Lloyd was in awe of the SAS operation, and felt it was timely to produce a film showing the elite unit in action.

Lloyd procured the services of former intelligence officer and writer George Markstein. The subject matter was topical and Lloyd was keen to offer an anti-terrorism message, but he and Markstein opted to make changes. The US embassy becomes the target in their story, and the Iranian extremists are substituted with anti-nuclear protesters. The treatment was written within a week, then passed to American writer Reginald Rose, who had previously worked on multi-star war/action thrillers like *The Wild Geese* and *The Sea Wolves*. *Who Dares Wins*, as

The terrorist guard sleeps, as General Potter (Robert Webber) attempts to grab the Uzi machine gun. Behind them is the American Secretary of State (Richard Widmark) - another VIP hostage held by the People's Lobby faction in the American Ambassador's London residence.

WHO DARES WINS

Lewis Collins as the SAS Captain, Peter Skellen.

WHO DARES WINS

Having abseiled from helicopters to the American Embassy residence roof, the SAS 'snipe' soldiers then abseil down the walls and explode their way in to the first floor rooms.

WHO DARES WINS

Lewis Collins as the SAS captain, Peter Skellen and Judy Davis as the terrorist he confronts, Frankie Leith.

WHO DARES WINS

Looking like evil spacemen, the SAS progress cautiously along the American Embassy residence passageways ready to shoot to kill. In an operation of this type against armed, fanatical terrorists, they don't aim to take prisoners.

WHO DARES WINS

the movie was titled (those three words being the motto of the SAS), was intended to be a similar beast, but the big names involved were relegated to supporting roles, like Richard Widmark as an American diplomat and Edward Woodward as a police chief. Lloyd's backers were willing to go with a smaller name actor as the leading man, a rising television star perhaps - Collins, of course, was perfect.

He'd been fascinated with parachuting since childhood visits to army ranges and signed up for lessons. This resulted in him breaking his ankle during a jump between filming episodes of *The Professionals*. Undeterred, he signed up for the Territorial Army Volunteer Reserves Parachute Regiment in 1979. He kept in shape through training with weights, dumb-bells and bench presses, also continuing with his Paras training and resumed martial arts, in particular ju-jitsu. In 1980, Collins went through his TAVR selection course and gained his Red Beret, joining the 10th Battalion (10 Para). He actually began the selection course for the TA branch of the SAS but was rejected as his celebrity profile had become too sizeable to accommodate the strict anonymity required by the unit. Nevertheless, he was undoubtedly fit and strong enough to have done it for real! Therefore, Collins was physically ideal for the role of Peter Skellen and extremely eager to do justice to the character.

He said: "The SAS are my heroes. They are men who have proved themselves physically fit in the extreme, they are intelligent and they're very discreet."

Immediately increasing his training regime, Collins was in tip-top condition by the time the *Who Dares Wins* press announcement took place in August 1981, having lost 25lb by quitting drinking and smoking and exercising rigorously.

All seemed set for another big

Euan Lloyd hit, one that would open Hollywood doors for Collins. He was backed by a strong cast which, as well as Widmark and Woodward, included Judy Davis, Robert Webber and a great selection of British television regulars including John Duttine, Ingrid Pitt, Tony Doyle, Nick Brimble, Maurice Roeves, Paul Freeman and Tony Osoba. Roy Budd contributed a wonderfully funky soundtrack and the whole thing was presided over by director Ian Sharp who, despite being relatively new to the game, had worked with Collins successfully on episodes of *The Professionals*.

According to Sharp, the script "needed a lot of work". He flew to the United States to work with Rose on it, but they "never got to a really strong plot." He did rewrite the action scenes though, but what there was of a script was concurrently novelised by thriller writer James Follett as 'The Tiptoe Boys'. This took around 30 days, and as each chapter was completed, it was posted to LA to enable Rose to complete a final screenplay. Despite these issues, a decent budget was raised by pre-selling the film to various overseas territories, including America where it was retitled *The Final Option* as the SAS motto would be unfamiliar Stateside. The result is a movie that divides opinion, but I belong to the sizable crowd that is very fond of it, perhaps because it was one of the first VHS rentals my schoolmates and I watched at our house back in the early '80s.

Nostalgia aside, the picture achieves the sort of sturdy British level of 'epic' that proliferated during the '70s and early '80s. It feels like there is money behind it, helped by the numerous exterior locations of London and beyond, plus plenty of interiors in larger, more striking areas rather than endless plainly decorated office walls. And the opening Peace March features hundreds of extras and looks genuinely large in scale.

And here is one of the divisive

elements of the film. It opens as a political thriller, but one that seems to espouse right-wing opinions. There seems to be a suggestion that the anti-nuclear brigade are naïve dreamers at best, dangerous terrorists at worst. Lloyd and Sharp were always bemused by this because the text clarifies very quickly that the extremists are hiding in plain sight, acting as standard CND-types, cuckoos in a nest of peaceful protestors. True, most of the heroic authority figures get the chance to foghorn the reasons for nuclear deterrents, belittle pacifists and highlight the untrustworthy, unstable nature of activists, so the right-wing message is there for all who wish to latch onto it. In the end though, *Who Dares Wins* is no more gung-ho or oversimplified in its plot and characters than most other Us vs Them war stories.

The script follows SAS Captain Peter Skellen (Collins), who appears to have been thrown out of the service for gross misconduct but is actually intent on infiltrating a radical political group in order to end their terrorist plans. Thus, the politics soon begin to merge into a tale of undercover operations, culminating in a big, impressive mission to rescue hostages and punish the antagonists.

The war elements are established as soon as the viewer accompanies visitors to an SAS training camp. This is a fascinating sequence, sort of a beefed-up version of James Bond's Q Department combined with *The Professionals*. Collins is first seen 7 minutes in, looking '80s cool in a leather jacket, all in black and sitting with arms folded at a table surrounded by shooting targets. Training soldiers burst in firing and our hero doesn't flinch for even a second. Collins has great screen presence - he's great with a glower but expressive too, and capable of the most mischievous of smiles. He can talk the talk *and* walk the walk.

True, the script itself is often wordy and spends an awful lot of time pontificating on the issue of anti-nuclear protests, political obfuscation and the need for strong action in the face of one's country's enemies. What saves this from becoming too dry or heavy is the regular returns to either SAS or terrorist training, undercover investigations and violent action. There is enough going on to give the effect of a well thought-out, if sometimes simplistic, plotline. There are helicopters, explosions, bursts of gunfire, big-scale location shoots amidst harsh yet stunning mountain scenery and the wince-inducing 'beasting' of two innocent men, and that is just in the initial SAS training sequences.

Skellen's undercover exploits involve a passenger hovercraft, sporty cars, trendy mews apartments and a smouldering affair (all part of the job, right?) between the infiltrator and the prominent activist played by Davis. This part plays out over scenes of a jealously whiny John Duttine (as Davis' second-in-command) and a passionately driven Ingrid Pitt who, in training the terrorists and holding Skellen's family hostage, puts in one of her best performances on screen.

This all helps to keep the atmosphere thickening until the blue touchpaper is lit in the final third and the SAS launch a two-pronged attack, one to rescue the Skellen family and the other to raid the American Embassy, rescuing the hostages and bringing the terrorists to justice. Patrick Allen cameos as a reassuringly old-school police chief and Richard Widmark gets the opportunity to shine in a lovely, grandstanding debate with Davis, well backed-up by Robert Webber's spikier ambassador.

There are highs and lows, of course. On the negative side, there is a depressingly one-sided representation of skinheads as bigoted thugs. The film takes for granted the false stereotype promoted by screen depictions of right-wing gangs during the late '70s and early '80s. This inaccurate representation seems to have been taken up and overused forevermore in Hollywood. But at least there are some characters with more depth (even if untapped), such as Kenneth Griffith's sympathiser vicar who sheds both tears and blood when violence erupts at a Rock against the Bomb festival. This scene is excellently staged and muddies the waters between the good and the bad, something that adds texture to proceedings.

Sometimes, the anti-bomb rhetoric allows the foe to be both intelligent and dangerous but the 'blue sky thinking' results in wishy-washy cliches which eventually set them up as panicking amateurs. When Duttine looks at Widmark and Webber and exclaims: "What a couple of dumb bastards", the camera is actually focused on Davis and Duttine, establishing without doubt which side the text is on.

Perhaps it's finally best to just focus on the action,

stunts and effects. The bravery of the captured police constable despite being battered relentlessly, the planning and execution of Skellen's family and the slow-burning tension leading to a sudden, violent burst of action. The entirety of the final climactic event is directly inspired by the Iranian Embassy siege, right down to one SAS soldier being set alight by an explosion and putting himself out before continuing on his mission. This is rousing stuff indeed, with epic music, SAS choppers taking off and soldiers crashing through windows.

Best of all, Collins convinces in every scene, whether charming the opposition, running dangerously through London traffic to evade surveillance or his infamous run down a never-ending corridor, firing his machine gun as he goes. He is always believable and has screen charisma by the bucketload. As a cinematic debut as leading man, Collins ticks every box here. He deserved to go much further. In fact, *Who Dares Wins* was one of the ten highest grossers at the British box office in 1982. Unfortunately, distribution issues in the States resulted in much less business over there. Lloyd had signed Collins to a three-film deal, including *Wild Geese II*, a further movie that would focus on the Falklands War between the UK and Argentina (rumour has it that this might've featured the return of the Skellen

character) and a location-based piece called *Macau*. However, none came to pass. Lloyd feared that it would be confusing to use Collins as different lead characters in two concurrent pictures so Scott Glenn got the role in *Wild Geese II* (1985), which would be Lloyd's final production credit. The other two projects simply fizzled out.

All was not lost though, as there had been several suggestions that Collins might make a good James Bond. By this time, Roger Moore was on a film-by-film contract and producer Albert Broccoli had made it known that he was actively speaking to potential replacements. Collins'

ideas for the character seemed to tie in with the Timothy Dalton template, the Daniel Craig one even more so, but it appeared to be too soon for the Bond team who were nervy about moving too far from the then tongue-in-cheek approach of the Moore era. Collins actually spoke to Broccoli but, as the actor later said: "I was in his office for five minutes, but it was really over for me in seconds… He found me too aggressive."

The rumours arose again in 1983 when Moore insisted that *Octopussy* would be his last Bond for sure. Collins was supposedly on the shortlist of replacements, but said: "I really don't know if I am in the running. I certainly haven't been approached by Broccoli. If they did approach me, I don't know what I would say - it really would depend on what was offered. If I had to sign a seven-year contract, I'd probably say 'No' just because I wouldn't want to be that tied down. I certainly wouldn't envy anyone taking over the role at this stage, especially if they kept to the same format. They would have to allow the next guy to be himself and bring what he has to offer to the role. And then, it would take at least two movies to convince the world you are Bond. Even so, I have to admit it would be fun."

It was academic. Moore changed his mind, and that was that. When interviewed in 1985, Collins insisted that he wouldn't want the role and hadn't been interviewed. A line was drawn under the subject as far as he was concerned and yet, for many fans of both Collins and Bond, this will forever remain a missed opportunity for all parties.

At this point, Collins' adventures on the big screen seemed to be over as quickly and spectacularly as they had started. He returned later in the decade in a trio of spaghetti war films, but his leading-man debut in *Who Dares Wins* would remain his career high point.

BROADCAST NEWS

by Rachel Bellwoar

Broadcast News is about the state of journalism in the '80s. More than that, though, it's about three people - Tom (William Hurt), Aaron (Albert Brooks) and Jane (Holly Hunter) - who end up working together in the same newsroom in Washington.

Had director James L. Brooks opened the film in the newsroom, it might be a different story. Tom, Aaron and Jane would be cogs in the machine. Instead, Brooks uses the opening and closing scenes of the movie to single out its three leads and make *Broadcast News* about their fates, not the fate of the fourth estate.

Journalism is changing in *Broadcast News*. The characters, however, mostly stay the same, and nowhere is this better illustrated than in the opening sequence, which introduces all three of them as children (played by Kimber Shoop, Dwayne Markee and Gennie James respectively) before transitioning to the present day. The idea is that these three individuals were born for the jobs they eventually have as adults.

In Tom's first scene, for example, we see him confessing to his father (Stephen Mendillo) about his grades and being constantly praised for his looks. Tom is a future news anchor. While he claims to be disturbed by how he's

being treated, the convincing nature of his 'performance' (which, we suspect, might be insincere) is the problem. We find ourselves wondering if his confession is genuine or if he is faking, giving a performance. Tom's father seems convinced, and that's really all we have to go on at this stage in the story. We have to rely on Tom's word and the fact that his father (who presumably knows him best) seems to think he is being too hard on himself. What doesn't come out until later is that Tom needs his father's signature for something. He is basically 'playing' the Old Man in order to get it. When his seemingly heartfelt confession works, Tom gets the signature, no problem.

Throughout *Broadcast News*, Tom never grows out of the habit of telling sob stories. The only difference is that Jane is usually the one subjected to them, though interestingly Tom's relationship with his father remains important. It's dad who Tom calls after his first story, and towards the end of the film he stops by for a visit with the Old Man. It's not just that Tom admires his father; it's that his father sympathizes with him and his plight as an unqualified white man who keeps getting jobs. Tom admires Jane, too, but whenever she questions him or won't take his 'woe be me' speeches seriously, he gets angry or walks away. By showing Tom as a child, *Broadcast*

63

News establishes that he has been giving people this spiel for years. He's all talk, no action. Yet it's telling that, even with this information, we feel an inclination to want to believe him, to trust that he's being sincere even though we know he probably isn't.

In the same way that Tom needed something from his father when he told him about his grades, his first interactions with Jane are also built around a lie. She thinks he's being kind to her when, after watching her bomb during a presentation, he tells her how much he enjoyed her talk. Director Brooks lets viewers think this too, by giving no indication that Tom has ulterior motives.

It's only when watching the film for a second time that Tom's deception really sinks in, because none of the characters really react to it. Basically, he deliberately seeks Jane out because he knows they are going to be co-workers. Regardless of that knowledge would've affected Jane's decision to pursue Tom romantically, he leaves her at a disadvantage while letting himself come across as a nice guy. The outrage over Tom's hiring, however, distracts Jane from reacting much to the deception, which is probably intentional. After all, Tom has to remain a viable love interest throughout the movie, so his faults can't be examined too closely.

If getting a glimpse at Tom's childhood helps establish behavior patterns for him, the years don't change Aaron and Jane much either. It's interesting that their personalities are a lot more similar. Aaron's high school graduation, for instance, goes about as well Jane's presentation in the present day (which goes about as well as Aaron's sweaty attempt to anchor the news). It's not that Jane and Aaron don't try to relate to people; it's that when they do, it usually sticks out like a sore thumb, such as when Jane pushes the microphone aside to try and better connect with her peers at the conference. The gesture is supposed to help create an open dialogue but, instead of looking natural, it reads like she is trying too hard.

Aaron and Jane can't do what Tom does, but he can't do what they do either. We see the difference in how *they* prep for a story (by cramming) versus how *Tom* preps (by picking out his shirt and tie). Aaron and Jane have to speak out against injustices. It's the reason Aaron relishes getting to expose his peers at graduation (he is a future reporter), and why Jane doesn't hesitate to correct her father (Leo Burmester) when he calls her obsessive (she's a future producer).

Usually, movies are invested in seeing the characters grow or change, but *Broadcast News* is more interested in whether its three leads can stay the same and be true to themselves. It's why the film's resolution is more realistic than romantic (a decision that works to the film's credit, even if it has its detractors). Doing the right thing is hard, and with that comes consequences. *Broadcast News* understands that the real drama is in seeing how Tom, Jane

and Aaron will fare against a changing world of journalistic ethics.

The way *Broadcast News* does this, though, is what makes it so special - its use of movement to convey the story. Usually 'choreography' is a term used to describe dancing, but in *Broadcast News* the way characters move within the space in the newsroom is extremely telling and revealing. On a basic level, there's the general hustle and bustle of the newsroom (most dramatically represented by Joan Cusack's iconic dash to get a tape in by deadline). But Brooks and cinematographer Michael Ballhaus also use space to convey power dynamics and internal struggles. Whether it's seeing a character in the foreground watch a character in the background, or having one character stand at a higher level than the other, there's always something to learn from where each character is positioned. *Broadcast News'* leads may be consistent but the frames are so layered it's impossible to get bored.

If one scene epitomizes this, it's when Aaron and Jane's fight after Aaron's disastrous attempt to anchor the news. In James L. Brooks' commentary with editor Richard Marks for the 2011 Criterion DVD release, he talks about having trouble finding the right location for Aaron's house. All of that effort pays off, though, because the layout of the house adds a lot to the sequence. From the front door, which leads to either the kitchen or a hallway, Jane and Aaron are given two options for entering the living room, and they take them - a decision that immediately sets the tone for their fight. The double entrances matter

because, instead of leaving, Jane always ends up going around in circles. Aaron is her friend so she can't just walk away. But Aaron is also a reporter and he has to tell her the truth. Because Jane is who she is, she has to listen. Journalism has nothing and everything to do with their fight. Aaron and Jane can't separate who they are from what they do. But, while their profession is fickle, Aaron and Jane are steadfast. That's why they (along with Tom) are what *Broadcast News* is really all about.

Living the Dream
FITZCARRALDO

by Jonathon Dabell

Occasionally, a film proves so extraordinarily difficult or troublesome to make that the behind-the-scenes story becomes as fascinating as the movie itself. Such tales of 'Production Hell' make you appreciate how arduous it can be to put together a motion picture. *Cleopatra* (1963), *Apocalypse Now* (1979) and *The Man Who Killed Don Quixote* (2018) are notable examples. The latter two, in fact, are the subject of amazing 'Making Of...' documentaries (*Hearts of Darkness: A Filmmaker's Apocalypse* (1991) and *Lost in La Mancha* (2002) respectively) which chronicle the trials and tribulations which took place behind the cameras.

Another movie which belongs in this category is Werner Herzog's *Fitzcarraldo* (1982), arguably the most strenuous-to-make film in motion picture history. The documentary *Burden of Dreams* (1982), directed by Les Blanks, details the extraordinary shooting story and makes for a mind-boggling watch. And *Fitzcarraldo* itself is remarkable - totally unique, utterly authentic, indeed one of my favourite films ever.

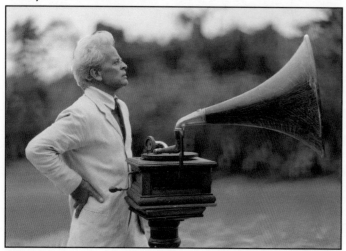

When Herzog was first urged to consider making a movie about an opera-loving rubber baron in turn-of-the-century Amazonia, he was reluctant to take it on. He didn't think the subject was particularly interesting and had no enthusiasm for it. He changed his mind after coming across a true story about an eccentric man who disassembled an entire ship into hundreds of parts, had the parts transported to a different river several miles away, then completely reassembled and refloated the vessel. Such tenacity and determination in the face of adversity intrigued Herzog, and he used it to formulate the seeds of a story.

The plot of *Fitzcarraldo* is fairly straightforward. An opera-loving Irishman named Brian Sweeney Fitzgerald (Klaus Kinski) lives in Iquitos, Peru, in the early 1900s. He is enraptured when he manages to see the great tenor Enrico Caruso performing at the newly built opera house in Manaus, Brazil. Manaus has until recently been nothing more than a primitive assortment of huts, sheds and ramshackle cabins on the banks of the mighty River Amazon. But the rubber boom has resulted in its rapid expansion, and it has become a city almost overnight, boasting proper buildings, a thriving population and even a grand opera house.

Fitzgerald, who goes by the name Fitzcarraldo (which is easier for the locals to pronounce), is determined to build a similar opera house in Iquitos. To fund it, he plans to make his fortune as a rubber baron. However, the only purchasable area of land he can find that will be suitable for a rubber plantation is in a remote location hundreds of miles upstream from Iquitos. It cannot be reached by land (due to impenetrable jungle) or river (due to unnavigable rapids). While studying a map, Fitzcarraldo spots another river running parallel to the unnavigable one, and notices

there is a point where both rivers almost meet, coming within a mile or so of each other beyond the rapids. He hits upon the ambitious idea of sailing down the 'better' river to the point where they almost meet, then dragging his ship across the dividing stretch of land to the other river. After an arduous voyage to reach the spot in question, he is dismayed to discover a huge hill full of trees and foliage lying on the piece of land that separates the two waterways. Contemplating failure, defeat and likely financial ruin, he decides to seek the help of seemingly hostile indigenous Indians to drag the ship over the hill. It is a desperate final throw of the dice - a wild plan, an impossible dream - but Fitzcarraldo's obsession with bringing opera to the jungle knows no bounds and he attempts it anyway.

When 20th Century Fox first heard about the project, they were interested in financing and distributing it. They spoke to Herzog about his requirements - what sets, storyboards, props and miniatures would he need to shoot the action? Herzog explained that he did not intend to make the film in such a way. No. His was a crazier plan. He was going to take his cast and crew to authentic Amazonian locations thousands of miles from civilisation, where they would attempt to drag a real steamship over a real hill in the real jungle. No matte paintings. No miniatures. No storyboards. No special effects. No clever trick photography. They would attempt to carry out the impossible feat just as the character of Fitzcarraldo attempts it in the story - for real.

Unsurprisingly, 20th Century Fox baulked at the idea and withdrew their interest. Indeed, many others felt Herzog was going too far in pursuit of authenticity and verisimilitude. Why, they wondered, was he so hell-bent on going so far into the jungle? Why drag a real ship over a real hill? Herzog explained that he was trying to create "a quality of force" that couldn't be faked. He wanted his audience to know they could trust their own eyes, to feel they were experiencing something unprecedented, something never-before-seen. He wanted them to witness scenes that were true and real which couldn't be artificially replicated. He was reaching for a richness and texture that simply couldn't be generated by shooting in a studio or close to civilisation.

As if all that wasn't challenging enough, the production seemed plagued by bad luck throughout. The early stages of production were already underway in 1979 when Herzog arranged for a camp to be built near the Ecuadorian/Peruvian border to house over a thousand cast, crew and technicians. But then news reached them that a small border war was brewing, making the area increasingly unsafe. It didn't help that the indigenous population were involved in a heated dispute of their own too over the exploitation of their land, and rumours began circulating that the film company would be committing all sorts of unsavoury acts during their stay - destroying the land, polluting the river, raping the women, smuggling arms and drugs, etc. Grim photographs from WWII, showing open mass graves piled high with the corpses of murdered Jews, were shown to the locals. They were told this was what Herzog's film company had done to another local community while making their film. This was 'disinformation' of the worst kind, and it was being used as a propaganda tool long before there was even a word for it. Shortly thereafter, Herzog's company was forced to vacate the region and abandon their first attempt to start work on the film.

Filming resumed in 1981 in a different location, with Jason Robards cast as Fitzcarraldo and Mick Jagger playing a sidekick character. Herzog told Jagger he could make more money by performing one night on stage than he would by spending several months in the jungle working on his film, but the rock star insisted he was willing to endure the misery and suffering because he truly loved the script. However, filming had only been in progress for a few weeks when Robards fell gravely ill and had to be flown back to America, where his doctor forbade him from returning to the shooting location. Once more, Herzog faced a delay while he sought a new leading actor. Jack Nicholson was one of the names considered then discarded, and at one point the director contemplated playing the role himself if a suitable replacement couldn't be found. Jagger reluctantly pulled out as he had a scheduling conflict due to a looming album tour, and Herzog was forced to write out the sidekick character completely. Eventually a new Fitzcarraldo was cast in the shape of three-time Herzog collaborator Klaus Kinski (they'd worked together on *Aguirre, the Wrath of God*, *Woyzeck* and *Nosferatu the Vampyre*). Kinski had been on the shortlist all along, but Herzog knew from experience that he was an incredibly temperamental man and had hoped to avoid casting him. He wanted to work with a more "rational" actor if possible.

The arrival of Kinski brought with it a whole new set of challenges and problems. Notoriously difficult, the actor had frequent tantrums and blazing rows with Herzog during shooting. The director required the patience of a saint to deal with these incredible rages from his volatile star. It got so bad that, at one point, a native Indian (a non-professional actor playing a member of the tribe) casually asked Herzog if he would like him to kill the abusive, foul-tempered actor. For many scenes, Herzog needed the character of Fitzcarraldo to appear calm and serene - benign in the midst of tumultuous events - and he knew it would be hard to draw that kind of performance from Kinski if he was in one of his usual foul moods. So, Herzog would deliberately provoke or trigger the actor and let him rant for a couple of hours until his nervous rage was spent. Then, when the actor had no energy left

to continue shouting and arguing, Herzog would shoot the scene and capture the kind of muted tranquillity he was looking for.

The biggest challenge of all involved the ship. It was not unheard of for ships to be moved from one waterway to another overland, but this was always done by disassembling the vessel, moving the parts, then putting it back together at the required location. The idea hatched by Fitzcarraldo the character (and Herzog the director) was to move the entire vessel intact over a jungle-infested hill. It was an unprecedented, untried feat. No-one really knew how it was going to turn out, or even if it was possible at all. It soon became apparent the ship could not be dragged up the 60-degree incline, even after it had been cleared of trees and foliage, so a huge Caterpillar bulldozer was brought in from Miami to reduce the steepness of the slope until it was closer to 40 degrees. Getting the Caterpillar to the location took weeks, and whenever it broke down under the immense strain of the task, there was a delay of days and weeks while repairs were carried out.

Two ships were used, both kitted out to look identical. While the slow and painstaking process of dragging one of them over the hill was being shot, the scenes showing the ship in motion, making its way upriver, were filmed simultaneously on the lookalike vessel. But even here there were problems, because at one point the mobile lookalike ship ran aground and was trapped in the shallows for months as the river level dropped because it was the dry season. Such delays were frequent, frustrating and lengthy; indeed, there were several points when the financial backers considered pulling out completely and it was only impassioned pleas and promises from Herzog that convinced them to stick with it.

After Fitzcarraldo manages to get the ship over the hill and into the parallel river, the natives (who believe him to be some sort of White God) mistakenly think it is his destiny to ride the ship down the rapids back to Iquitos. They do not understand he specifically wants to be upriver from the rapids as this is where he will work the land for

rubber. It is one of the great ironies of the story that all Fitzcarraldo's efforts are for nothing. His ship ends up being cut loose by the natives on the other river because they believe, incorrectly, that they have dragged the ship over the hill for him so he can show his superiority by riding it through the rapids. They cut if free and look on as it drifts back downstream toward the very rapids Fitzcarraldo has toiled so desperately to avoid.

To shoot the sequence where the ship drifts into the rapids and is tossed around helplessly - smashing into rocks, thudding against the embankment, pitching and rolling in the swell, its bow sometimes underwater - Herzog came up with his craziest idea of all. He decided to put his cast and cameramen aboard the vessel and get them to ride the rapids for real. A worried Kinski challenged the director to be aboard with them, and Herzog agreed that he could only expect them to do it if he was willing to be by their side. Not knowing if the ship would survive the ride, Herzog, Kinski and crew rode it into the swell and let nature takes its course. The resulting footage is, of course, incredible. The crashing and scraping sounds are authentic; the dizzying motion of the vessel genuine; and when the actors are thrown across the deck during its wild spins and collisions, it's all for real. It came at a cost too - one cameraman was flung thirty feet across the deck while holding his camera, landing with such force that the weight of the camera split his hand apart. Almost everyone came out with bumps, cuts, or bruises... but somehow, against all odds, they made it through and captured their remarkable, one-of-a-kind footage.

Inevitably, Herzog was accused of recklessness and endangering lives. He maintains to this day that there are a lot of inaccurate myths surrounding the making of the film, that it was more disciplined than reports suggest and that most of the risks taken were calculated not life-threatening. By the time shooting wrapped, he was so overwhelmed and exhausted - drained of all emotion - that he felt numb. There was no catharsis, no sense of achievement, no relief that all the footage was finally in the can - just a sense of emptiness, a detached realisation that filming had come to an end.

Of course, it's hard to justify lives being put at risk for the sake of making a movie. But putting those concerns aside for a moment, *Fitzcarraldo* is a breathtaking film - a fever dream on one hand and an inspirational story of ambition and determination on the other. The ship being pulled over a seemingly insurmountable hill is spectacular to watch, but it also works a grand metaphor. "Dream!" it screams, "fulfil it! Do it! Make the impossible happen! Faith and determination move mountains." It is, in essence a film about pursuing one's dreams, no matter how crazy they are. Herzog himself did not fully realise this until the movie was completed, and admitted he hadn't initially set out to make a film with this as its central theme. Nevertheless, it's what he ended up with.

No other movie contains scenes like it, because nothing had ever been shot this way before nor since. It's a unique experience, visually enthralling as you'd expect but also enthralling as a story about human obsession and determination.

Kinski is superb as the title character. Even knowing how diabolically he behaved behind the scenes, one feels nothing but admiration for the way he performs in front of the camera. Rough footage remains of the Robards and Jagger version, which looks interesting and somewhat different from the film as it turned out. It has to be said that Kinski brings a riveting dimension to it and it's hard to imagine anything or anyone bettering the version that was ultimately released. Undoubtedly, *Fitzcarraldo* with Robards and Jagger would have been a good, possibly great, film… but there's no point ruing that it was never made because what we got in its place is so exceptional.

As extraordinary as dragging the ship over the hill and riding it through rapids are, two of my favourite scenes were actually much simpler to put together. One takes place as the ship enters hostile Indian waters and an ominous silence weighs heavily on everyone's senses. Fearing they are being watched, that they may be ambushed or speared at any moment, those aboard stare apprehensively into the jungle which seems to reach for them from the riverbank. Fitzcarraldo cannot stand the tension any longer so heads to the top deck with his gramophone, where he starts playing Caruso at full volume, letting the tenor's incredible

GAUMONT présente

Fitzcarraldo

Un film de WERNER HERZOG

KLAUS KINSKI
CLAUDIA CARDINALE
dans "Fitzcarraldo" Un film de W. HERZOG
avec JOSE LEWGOY, MIGUEL ANGEL FUENTES
PAUL HITTSCHER, HUERE...QUE ENRIQUE BOHORQUEZ
GRANDE OTHELO, PETER BERLING
Images de THOMAS MAUCH, Musique de POPOL VUH
Produit par WERNER HERZOG et LUCKI STIPETIC
Une Coproduction WERNER HERZOG FILMPRODUKTION et PROJECT FILMPRODUKTION

RETURN TO OZ

by Simon J. Ballard

In 1985, not many people knew the name L. Frank Baum. And those that did weren't necessarily aware he'd written a whole series of books set in the land of Oz. Most might only have heard of the first one, 'The Wonderful Wizard of Oz', which appeared in 1900 and was famously filmed in 1939. The film *Return to Oz* (1985) was looked upon by viewers as nothing more than a sequel - a rather late one at that - to 1939's glorious, magical Technicolor musical *The Wizard of Oz*, when in actual fact it was an adaptation of an entirely different Baum book. In some ways, this rather dark fantasy was doomed from the start. Its critical and box office performance was unimpressive, and viewers largely failed to grasp what it was trying so desperately *not* to be.

This is a great shame, for it sits rather comfortably in hindsight alongside other fantasy-adventure pics from the same era like *The Dark Crystal*, *Labyrinth* and *Willow*. Since the film was released by Disney, perhaps audiences were expecting something thematically a little lighter, more supposedly child friendly.

I'm probably being slightly simplistic here, as there's no way the makers genuinely expected viewers to forget the 1939 original. That would be quite ridiculous, as it was a long-established classic and firmly rooted in everyone's conscience. However, the director and co-writer Walter Murch wanted to emulate the look and feel of Baum's original books, which were a world and a rainbow away from Victor Fleming's all-singing, all-dancing parade of

colour and delight. Fleming's original *The Wizard of Oz* was a handy stepping-stone in the sense that it allowed Murch to bring to life the characters and stories from the second and third of Baum's books, 'The Marvellous Land of Oz' and 'Ozma of Oz', written in 1904 and 1907 respectively. He got the chance to direct after making a name for himself doing sound editing on George Lucas' *THX 1138* and *American Graffiti*, as well as *The Godfather* for Francis Ford Coppola. This proved significant, which I'll come to later.

It's worth noting Murch wasn't the first to come up with the notion of adapting more of Baum's books for the screen. It's just that he was able to see it through to the end, just about, where others had failed. Way back in 1954, Walt Disney Pictures had acquired the rights to the remaining Oz books and set about making a production that would have been called *Rainbow Road to Oz*, but the film (part of a proposed TV series) was never completed and for decades the rights just sat gathering dust.

The story concocted by Murch from the above-mentioned books (aided by co-writer Gill Dennis) catches up with a red-eyed, sleep-deprived Dorothy (Fairuza Balk) six months after her adventures in Oz. Unable to sleep and unable to stop talking to Auntie Em and Uncle Henry about her adventures with the Scarecrow, Tin Woodsman and Cowardly Lion, Dorothy becomes a victim (sorry, patient) of Dr Worley (Nicol Williamson) who uses electroconvulsive therapy to try to zap memories of Oz

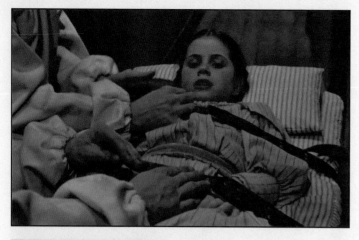

away. We soon realise Dorothy is considered mentally ill because she talks about Oz all the time and believes the place and its inhabitants to be real. During a storm, a rather handy power cut occurs and Dorothy escapes thanks to the plucky help of a fellow inmate (sorry, patient). Soon, she finds herself… well, somewhere rather familiar.

Balk, at ten years of age, is a fully capable and engrossing performer to watch, especially during the scenes at Worley's sanitorium (I guess I should say 'hospital', but 'sanitorium' is much closer to the truth, especially with the sounds of groaning emanating from the cellar!) The hospital scenes contain some the darkest material you'll find in the name of family entertainment, such as Dorothy being strapped to a gurney with squeaky wheels by two grim-faced orderlies under the orders of the cold Head Nurse (Jean Marsh). Worley is played with geniality by Williamson, but that geniality wears off when he uses a machine with a creepy mechanical face to flood Dorothy's brain with happy, go-away thoughts.

Murch may have claimed that *Return* was not to be viewed as a direct sequel to *Wizard*, but he does repeat one trope from the earlier movie by having characters from Kansas appear as parallel characters in Oz. Thus, Williamson is the main adversary when the action moves to Oz, appearing as the stony-faced, stony-bodied Nome King. Likewise, Marsh plays the frightening, head-swapping Princess Mombi during the Oz scenes. And the bare-footed girl is the captured Princess Ozma (Emma Ridley, dubbed by Murch's daughter Beatrice). The pumpkin she gives Dorothy as an early Hallowe'en gift later manifests into the kindly but clumsy Jack Pumpkinhead, and the orderlies from the hospital are 'Ozified' as the fearsome but rather ineffectual Wheelers, whose hands and feet are replaced by wheels (yeah, sounds daft… but when I saw this at the cinema on release, aged six, they made me and most of the other kids in the audience cower in our seats). Even the slow-winding clockwork dial on Worley's machine is paralleled as Tik-Tok, a brass-patented mechanical man who needs winding up to think, speak and move. Spare a thought for gymnast and *Blue Peter* presenter Michael Sundin, who was strapped inside Tik-Tok, often upside-down or back to front!

A forlorn and mournful atmosphere pervades Oz as Dorothy explores. Her dog Toto from the original is replaced here with a talking chicken named Billina, 'played' by forty real animals plus one highly impressive mechanical model (which looked so real that it fooled many a crew member). Stepping on stones to avoid the Deadly Desert (one touch, you turn to sand), Dorothy is unaware her arrival has been noted by a number of stones bearing a single eye or a face. Her presence is reported back to the Nome King, who, for reasons as yet unknown, forbids chickens in his realm.

At one point, Dorothy finds the house in which she

made her journey in the tornado in the original book and film. In this scene, it feels like we're turning the pages of a fairy tale as well as experiencing a Proustian rush for those who adore *Wizard*. There is also genuine sadness to be felt when we see the Yellow Brick Road all broken up and festooned with weeds. In fact, the whole of Oz is rendered a ransacked ruin thanks to some gorgeous matte paintings. We learn that all the emeralds in the land have been stolen by the Nome King and the populace have been turned to stone (including the Tin Woodsman and the Cowardly Lion). Interestingly, the Tin Man in *Return* (like the Scarecrow) is designed in such a way that he doesn't resemble the character from 1939 production, but rather one from the original cover of the book 'The Marvellous Land of Oz.'

Despite her dominance of the screen for much of *Return*, Balk was only allowed to shoot for around three-and-a-half hours a day due to her age. She really is incredibly capable. Her sadness at the state of Oz is keenly felt, as well as her fear during the scene where Mombi casually swaps one head for another in a gallery of heads behind glass cabinets. This scene is magnificently creepy, and many a youngster has been scared to death by it over the years. Balk interacts well with her newfound friends Tik-Tok and Jack Pumpkinhead (played by Brian Henson, son of Jim), a tall, gangly figure constantly in danger of falling apart and desperate to find his mom. I love it when Jack

expresses surprise or fear, causing his head to narrow in lieu of actual facial expressions.

There is some gorgeous set design work by Norman Reynolds which deserves a mention. The faded splendour of the surrounds of Oz contrasts with the opulence of Mombi's palace, her throne room a glittering display of polished mirrors from floor to ceiling. Once Dorothy reaches the Nome King's mountain, with a little help from the head of a gump lashed to two chaise-longues and liberally sprinkled with Mombi's powder of life, we are treated to a view of the domain of the King which resembles the real-life Giant's Causeway in Northern Ireland. The set is augmented with Claymation hands which claw away to make a doorway, as well as breathing life into the features of the King himself, at first voiced then embodied by Williamson.

Rather cruelly, the King has transformed the Scarecrow into an ornament. Dorothy and her friends are told that if they can find the right ornament, he will be transformed back to his proper self. However, each false guess will result in the guesser being transformed into an ornament themselves. Not only that, but every time someone chooses wrongly, the King becomes slightly more human, less of a stone-like entity. As her friends are sent one by one to guess and make bad choices, we really sense the pathos in Dorothy as she loses them. Balk is great in this scene, conveying richly expressive empathy.

There was one element from the 1939 movie that people are often surprised to learn was never in any of the books - the ruby slippers. They were originally silver, but rubies were naturally felt more colourful for the screen adaptation. Therefore, Disney had to pay a substantial fee to MGM to be allowed to use the ruby slippers in this 1985 version. In a key scene, the Nome King taunts Dorothy by, er, wearing the slippers himself. Okay, fair enough, they have magical properties and he is made of malleable stone. But it doesn't disguise the fact they look damn silly on him, even in this age of ever-increasing gender-fluid clothing choices!

The costume worn by Williamson, along with his make-up, really evoke a feeling of slate and stone. I may be wrong, but I'm not sure he ever blinks when he is in shot, merely narrowing his eyes into a stony look of evil. It's a powerhouse performance, his already richly deep voice given greater post-production resonance.

I mentioned earlier that Murch only just got *Return to Oz* made. In fact, when the shooting schedule began to slide and when the Disney executives expressed dissatisfaction about the footage already shot, he was fired five weeks in. Funnily enough, the 1939 *Wizard* went through three directors before Victor Fleming was brought on board, and even then King Vidor finished off some of the last remaining scenes. Murch may well have been replaced permanently had it not been for the vote of confidence shown in him by Lucas and Coppola, which was sufficient to get him reinstated. Lucas even offered to finish the shoot if Murch prove unwilling or unable. But return he did, managing to complete the movie the way he wanted, Alas, the poor returns - less than half the $28 million budget - saw to it that he would never direct another feature.

The one element the critics latched onto most, apart from the obvious comparison to the 1939 original, was the remarkably dark tone of *Return*. This was actually a creative decision to make the film contrast markedly with MGM's epic. Many claimed it was far too dark and scary for youngsters to take. Certain elements certainly frightened me as a child, such as the Wheelers (look, I said I was only six, okay!?), head-swapping Mombi and the terrifying Nome King. But nevertheless, I became obsessed with the feature despite being somewhat scared by it. Its spirit of adventure is there front and centre, and many ideas from Baum's books are brought vividly to life with great practical effects which broaden the scope of the picture. Recently, Neil Gaiman declared it: "one of the very best fantasy films I've ever seen."

In Fairuza Balk, we have a protagonist we can care about and sympathise with, and the story introduces a motley crew to help her along in their own fun, haphazard way. Admittedly, it does feel rather criminal to render Dorothy's pals from *Wizard* into little more than cameos, and the climax feels a little rushed. No sooner has Dorothy met the now freed Princess Ozma - Jack's real mom, so to speak - than she is cast back home. But was it all a dream? On reflection, it would prove not to be thanks to a visitation from Ozma through the mirror on Dorothy's dresser back in Kansas, where there's no place for Nomes. But, abrupt ending aside, this is an '80s fantasy classic and well worth a look.

THE COLOR OF MONEY
...and Getting Used

by Sebastian Corbascio

Martin Scorsese makes movies that are like operas. He grew up in Little Italy in New York City, a crowded, vibrant neighbourhood where music of every description drifted out of open brownstone windows, competing to be heard. One could walk one block and hear opera crossfading into rock n' roll crossfading into Motown, and so on - sounds that are familiar to any Scorsese acolyte. With the exception of *After Hours* and *The King of Comedy*, two comic projects with tighter studio control and smaller needle-drop budgets, Scorsese made operas. *The Color of Money* is no exception.

When it was released, the film grossed $52.3 million at the box office. Poolhalls started doing an astounding amount of business and Warren Zevon's song *Werewolves of London* became a hit again. *The Color of Money* was supposed to be Scorsese's comeback picture as well as a commercial studio movie that would hopefully earn enough money to enable him to get approval to make *The Last Temptation of Christ*. It delivered seven-time nominee Paul Newman his first ever Oscar. It has jaw-dropping scenes, and, as mentioned, brought songwriter Warren Zevon renewed attention. And yet it has faded into relative obscurity and rarely gets discussed alongside Scorsese's other work, nor Newman's or Cruise's for that matter. What the hell happened?

The Color of Money takes place 25 years after - and is a sequel to - *The Hustler* (1961), a classic jewel of American kitchen sink drama. *The Hustler* was about un-permanent people drifting along to the beck of America's open roads, knowing there is no destination except mobility itself. They were drifters, petty criminals, con artists, off-the-

grid kooks, the kind of people we might once have called 'rolling stones', the kind immortalized in Kerouac's 'On the Road' and in Kerouac himself. They can also be found in many a road movie. In 1986, the year *The Color of Money* arrived, the kind of guys who hung around at bus lockers while drifting from place to place were still around, but they were vanishing fast along with their haunts.

The film opens by reuniting us with one of the veterans of impermanence, 'Fast' Eddie Felson (Paul Newman), the main character from *The Hustler*. It seems he has maybe, sorta, settled down, but we soon learn that's not the case. In the intervening twenty-five years, he has re-invented himself as a liquor salesman, gleaning profits mainly by filling premium bottles with less premium stock and slinging on fake labels. You get the sense he is probably into more than a few other small rackets. He also acts as a stakehorse for minor pool hustlers like the coked-out Julian (John Turturro) in the ungentlemanly game of 9-ball. 9-ball is a fast-moving version of pool, perfect for the modern age and not like old-school pool, which was more a gentleman's game.

Eddie discovers Vincent Lauria (Tom Cruise), a brash, immature but prodigiously talented pool player with not much of a brain. Mary Elizabeth Mastrantonio plays Vincent's girlfriend Carmen. She is seasoned but is still open to new lessons in the hustling lifestyle from the great master himself. Her own hustle is decent enough: she still wears the amulet she stole from Vincent's mother, though Vincent naively doesn't realise it. ("He says his mother has one just like it," she explains). But Carmen isn't quite the bad-ass mama she thinks she is. In an early scene, Eddie bets with Vincent and Carmen that he can leave the bar with a seemingly random woman within ten minutes. Carmen ought to realise immediately that the woman at the bar already knows Eddie, but she only catches on much later. Carmen, like Vincent, is clay.

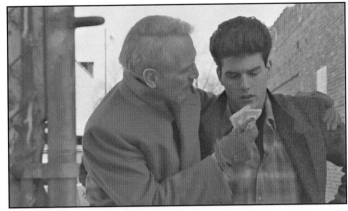

Eddie suggests that Carmen is "packing her bags" in an effort to control Vincent's showboating and all-round bullshit. Carmen tries to push Eddie's buttons by appearing nude in the bathroom mirror behind the oblivious Vincent. In another scene, she answers the door to Eddie scantily dressed. Eddie throws her around and tells her nothing is going to happen between them, that it would only screw up their long-term goals. Unlike most movies, this vamp doesn't pay the price for male ambition.

Eddie takes the couple with him on some poolhall cons, and they clean up. Eddie deliberately puts Vincent in a few nasty close shaves, but still Vincent doesn't seem to get it (though Carmen does). In fact, Vincent is a chump without Carmen. It begs the question: what would Carmen do without Vincent?

Eddie lets Vincent and Carmen go after he gets creamed at his own game by hustler Amos (Forrest Whittaker), a guy who's about a third of Eddie's age. The reason Eddie doesn't dump Vincent and offer to stakehorse Amos instead is that Eddie has nothing to teach him. Amos is already a damn good hustler - he hands Eddie his rear-end, and Eddie realises he is incomplete, that his life is at the tables. Everything else is secondary.

The Color of Money is a curious reversal of Scorsese's later *Gangs of New York* (2002) and several other films that make use of the student-kills/defeats-mentor tropes. Eddie needs Vincent to resurrect himself. At the end of the film, Vincent has a tantrum. "You used us!" he cries, finally understanding that Eddie's perceived affection for him was never there. Vincent was simply a go-cart. He may by now be a semi-seasoned hustler, but Vincent still failed to see Eddie's hustle until he was handed back the 8000 dollars he gave to Eddie for 'dumping' their tournament game. To a hustler, this is a stick in the eye. Vincent was never giving Eddie his best game.

The film's most famous scene is when Vincent steals away to play at Chalkie's, beating the best player in the poolhall but scaring off a potentially wealthier mark in the process. Zevon's *Werewolves of London* is the music used to score this scene. It aims for maximum iconography, and Scorsese delivers. The fluid camera acts like a dance partner for Vincent as he destroys his adversary Mozelle and, with it, anything remotely resembling his career as a pool hustler. "That boy's hot," one of Chalkie's whales comments, as the young prodigy dons his jacket and leaves with a fat roll of betting money. We realise Vincent can never succeed as a hustler until he learns to curb his ego. If Vincent had slayed the opposition anywhere but Chalkie's, it would have spelled the end of the big tournaments and

their lucrative back-room games.

The song *Werewolves of London* is significant because it tells the story of a well-dressed werewolf who kills and mutilates. As his legend grows, so does a dance craze surrounding him. It was born from fifteen minutes of Zevon, LeRoy Marinell and uber session man Waddy Wachtel screwing around in the studio. Don Everly had just seen the film *Werewolf of London* (1935) and threw the title out there to the trio to accompany what they had written. The song fits perfectly inside Zevon's ouvre of brutal tongue-in-cheek rock noir masterpieces, such as *Lawyers, Guns and Money*, *Poor Pitiful Me* and *Piano Fighter*, but *Werewolves* has one of the catchiest hooks in pop history, perfect for both bars and bar mitzvahs.

Much of the language used in the Way of the Hustle is buried - screenwriter Richard Price and Scorsese give no guidebook of hustling terminology, just enough for us to be able to keep playing catch-up. What makes us feel off-center is that Eddie, Carmen and Vincent are conning each other at all times. Or are they? We're not sure, and we never find out for sure.

Roger Ebert gave *The Color of Money* a scathing review. He was waiting for the final pool game between Vincent and Eddie, but this film's version of a Rocky .vs. Apollo Creed final clash never comes. Nor was it ever going to. Maybe Ebert is more oblivious than the rest of us, but it is pretty clear that the rivalry between Eddie and Vincent isn't their skill at the pool table, it's their skill on the take. There is no way that either of them will get their best game out of each other. If they ever do, neither would be the wiser.

Maybe *The Color of Money* needed a *Goodfellas*-type voice-over. Much of *Goodfellas* is an instructional film on the day-to-day Mob grind. If *The Color of Money* had a voiceover to explain the nuances of betting, taking the other guy's shirt, how to ride human greed all the way to the stash hole, it might help those viewers who don't get the language. In *Casino* (1995), Scorsese

went full tilt in the exposition, which was one of the many things its detractors disliked about it, though in recent years *Casino* has deservedly begun to get street cred all its own.

At the end of *The Color of Money*, Eddie can still hustle. His forfeiture of a pinnacle game shows that the old guy has a few tricks up his sleeve: the players will be lining up to play the legend in the back rooms because he's cunningly set up the perception that he's lost his touch. Younger guys will want to get a taste of what it's like to play and bet against a legend whose sun has set but who's still breathing. Felson can run into another Amos and take him over and over again. In the end, he lets Vincent know that he'll never know if he's getting Eddie Felson's best game, that Vincent will never know if he's truly beaten the master, nor will he be truly be sure if he's good enough to do so.

The Color of Money got Scorsese studio leverage; Tom Cruise got to check off another great director he wanted to work with, (a decade later, he would work with Stanley Kubrick too); Paul Newman got an Oscar; the film earned $52M theatrically ($2 million more than *Goodfellas*); and Warren Zevon went on to make the studio album *Sentimental Hygiene*, featuring some of music's greats. In fact, everyone who had a hand in *The Color of Money* came away richer. But, as a Scorsese work, it barely blips. So, what gives? Maybe *The Color of Money* cleaned up at the first round, everyone got what they wanted and, like any hustler who knows the craft, exited when the action cooled. Or maybe not. Who knows? Maybe you, the viewer, got used. Either way, it's all in the hustle.

by David Michael Brown

By 1980, Brian De Palma was in dire need of a hit. Success was an important touchstone for the director. His colleagues Steven Spielberg, George Lucas, Martin Scorsese and Francis Ford Coppola - the so-called 'movie brats' - had all seen their careers go from strength to strength. De Palma's 1976 adaptation of the Stephen King telekinetic coming-of-age tome 'Carrie' had earned the director commercial and critical accolades (as well as garnering Oscar nominations for Sissy Spacek and Piper Laurie) but De Palma was still not quite in the big league.

Carrie had topped a dream run artistically. *Sisters* (1972), *Phantom of the Paradise* (1974) and *Obsession* (1976) showed a director honing his craft, building on his infatuation with the cinema of Alfred Hitchcock. *The Fury* (1978) followed, starring Kirk Douglas, John Cassavetes and Amy Irving. De Palma took John Farris's source material and fashioned a Grand Guignol thriller that upped *Carrie*'s mind games with an explosive splash of gore and a stunning soundtrack by legendary composer John Williams.

His subsequent film school experiment *Home Movies* (1979) may have featured his *The Fury* star Douglas and Nancy Allen who played Carrie White's bitchy nemesis Kris, but it barely registered at the box office. So, the '70s had been artistically fulfilling for De Palma, but it was only *Carrie* that had proven a success. It was a return to his Hitch obsession that changed everything as the director entered a new decade.

Dressed to Kill (1980)

Despite paint-throwing feminists, scissor-happy censors and the perennial Hitchcock copyist accusations, *Dressed to Kill* was De Palma's biggest hit since *Carrie*. After years

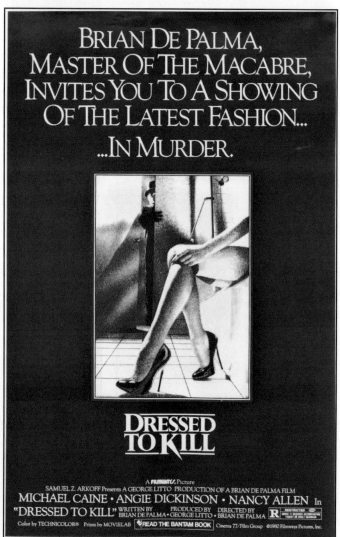

BRIAN DE PALMA, MASTER OF THE MACABRE, INVITES YOU TO A SHOWING OF THE LATEST FASHION... ...IN MURDER.

DRESSED TO KILL

A FILMWAYS Picture
SAMUEL Z. ARKOFF Presents A GEORGE LITTO PRODUCTION OF A BRIAN DE PALMA FILM
MICHAEL CAINE · ANGIE DICKINSON · NANCY ALLEN In
"DRESSED TO KILL" WRITTEN BY BRIAN DE PALMA PRODUCED BY GEORGE LITTO DIRECTED BY BRIAN DE PALMA
Color by TECHNICOLOR® Prints by MOVIELAB READ THE BANTAM BOOK Cinema 77/Film Group ©1980 Filmways Pictures, Inc.

of trying to live up to the telekinetic terrors of his Stephen King adaptation, it was the brazen sexuality and razor-slashing violence of his mean-spirited, transgender *Psycho* re-think that won audience favour.

At that point in his career, De Palma had hoped his next movie was going to be an adaptation of Gerald Walker's novel 'Cruising'. That film was eventually made by William Friedkin starring Al Pacino in 1980. De Palma retained the central conceit of people cruising for sex in *Dressed to Kill*.

A bravura piece of filmmaking that shamelessly plays on the rotund *Psycho* director's tried and tested traits, *Dressed to Kill* stars Angie Dickinson as a frustrated housewife who, after an illicit encounter in an art gallery, is viciously slashed to death in an elevator. Toying with audience expectations and showing off the director's predilection for split screens, forced perspectives and ultra-violence, the shocking murder is a master class in sustained tension.

The suburbanite who finds herself lying in a pool of her own blood is Kate Miller, played by Angie Dickinson. It was a shock to many to see the beloved *Police Woman* star not only brutally slashed to death but also naked in the shower during a rape fantasy sequence during the film's lurid opening moments. The frustrated housewife is killed after an afternoon dalliance with a random museumgoer. The seduction scene was shot at the Philadelphia Museum of Art - masquerading as New York's Metropolitan Museum of Art - and is a stunning sequence. For 10 minutes with no dialogue, De Palma's camera prowls behind Dickinson while Italian composer Pino Donaggio's stunning score swells in an audacious sequence that pays more than a

passing resemblance to Jimmy Stewart stalking Kim Novak in *Vertigo* (1958).

The main witness to the brutal murder is high-class prostitute Liz Blake (Nancy Allen) who becomes implicated in the crime. The part was written for Allen by her then husband De Palma. She explained in an interview with 'Speakeasy' what happened after the pair made *Home Movies* together: "He was at that point writing *Dressed to Kill*. Every day he got up really early in the morning, maybe three, and he'd go downstairs and write for a few hours. I'd come down for coffee and breakfast, and he'd read me the next instalment, and it was just... I mean, honestly, that script changed almost not one bit from the original draft. You could see it. It was so visual and the characters were so well-drawn for this type of film, obviously not a character piece. He finished it right around the time I was finishing up with *1941* (1979) and he said: 'What do you think?' I said: 'I think it's fantastic. It's a big, great movie.' He asked me what I thought of Liz, and I said: 'She's amazing.' He said: 'Well, that's your part.' Immediately I got very excited and then I thought, oh my God, how am I going to do this? This is like my first leading role."

While there is no doubt that the set-up is unashamedly Hitchcockian, the finale, as a scantily clad Allen seduces Michael Caine, playing psychiatrist Dr. Robert Elliott, is far more salacious. She uses her sexuality to secrete information from the doctor's diary while Kate's son Peter (Keith Gordon) watches helplessly through a window. Electronics nerd Peter has been using his tech knowledge to help Liz solve the crime. The character of Peter is based on the director himself, as De Palma told 'The New York Times': "That character in *Dressed to Kill* is me. I mean, that's my room. That machine, I built that machine."

Combining the blood-soaked thrills and askew sexuality of the giallo slashers with Hitch's talent for terror, *Dressed to Kill* is an astonishing exercise in pure cinema. The exploitative thriller also remains one of the director's most problematic exercises. Accusations of misogyny and

transphobia are still levelled at this beautifully crafted chiller to this day but, despite the controversy, *Dressed to Kill* remains a macabre masterpiece.

Blow Out (1981)

Blow Out was the political conspiracy thriller that followed. By avoiding the column-inch generating controversy of *Dressed to Kill* - or, perhaps, not generating enough - it arrived as something unwanted by audiences. Revisiting the thriller now, it's easy to see why many hail *Blow Out* as the New York director's masterpiece. With nods to Michelangelo Antonioni's *Blow-up* (1966), Francis Ford Coppola's *The Conversation* (1974) and the actual events at Chappaquiddick that rocked the United States, paranoia-drenched *Blow Out* stars John Travolta - a superstar since *Saturday Night Fever* (1977) - as Jack Terry, a jaded film sound technician who becomes embroiled in the fallout of a political scandal when he accidentally captures the assassination of a presidential candidate on tape while out recording sounds for a schlocky slasher he is working on called *Co-Ed Frenzy*.

Nancy Allen co-stars as Sally, the naïve eyewitness who Jack pulls from a sinking car. Jack and Sally are the first characters that cold and calculating De Palma appears to genuinely care about. After casting his partner as a conniving high-school bitch and a

high-class hooker with an eye on Wall Street, Allen was now playing a big-hearted innocent, despite being easily led astray by Dennis Franz's sleazy photographer. It wasn't always her role. When Travolta was cast, one over-enthusiastic executive wanted to line up an ill-advised *Grease* reunion by casting Olivia Newton-John.

"When I read it," explained Travolta to 'Films & Filming', "I just thought of Nancy immediately. Sally was perfect for her. But Brian and Nancy had made this pact not to work together so soon after *Dressed to Kill*. I just said to Brian: 'I really feel it's a mistake for Nancy not to play Sally.' At first, when Brian was thinking of [Al] Pacino or [Richard] Dreyfuss, he figured to cast someone like Dyan Cannon or Julie Christie in the part. But with me playing Jack, it really did make more sense to bring Sally's age closer to mine. Nancy and I had worked together before and the chemistry was so good between us, I just knew we'd be perfect together."

Blow Out, in fact, continued many relationships for the director. Travolta had appeared in *Carrie* as the boyfriend of Allen's teen vamp. John Lithgow, returning to the De Palma fold after playing the bad guy in *Obsession*, is creepy incarnate as Burke, the lobbyist who pushes things

too far, covering his tracks as the 'Liberty Bell Killer' years before he became the 'Trinity Killer' in *Dexter*. *Obsession* was also the first time De Palma had worked with legendary cinematographer Vilmos Zsigmond who returns for *Blow Out*, giving the film a beautiful, warm glow which accentuates De Palma's split-screen trickery and masterful use of the split focus diopter. The score marked De Palma's fourth collaboration with Pino Donaggio, the Italian composer behind the music for *Carrie*, *Dressed to Kill* and De Palma's New York film school experiment *Home Movies*. *Blow Out*'s most famed fan, Quentin Tarantino, used the aching piano-led track, Sally and Jack, on the soundtrack for *Death Proof* (2007).

The finale, as Jack pursues Sally (who has been wired by the sound guy) and the psychotic Burke through the streets of Philadelphia during the city's Liberty Bell parade is as tragic as it is heart-stopping. Tragedy also hit the shoot when two cartons containing 2,000 feet of uncut negative, including crucial footage of the parade chase,

were stolen from a shipping company van parked on 48th Street near the Avenue of the Americas in New York. After desperately searching for the footage in dumpsters and trash cans around Time Square, De Palma begrudgingly made the difficult decision to recall thousands of movie extras, cameramen and technicians to Philadelphia to reshoot the complex scene at a cost of $750,000 to the production's insurance company. This new footage was shot by *New York, New York* (1977) cinematographer László Kovács as Zsigmond was unavailable.

If you ever wondered why Tarantino cast Travolta in *Pulp Fiction*, then watch *Blow Out*. The film belongs to him. Noted critic Pauline Kael said of the film's performances in her 'New Yorker' review that: "Travolta finally has a role that allows him to discard his teenage strutting and his slobby accents" and that Allen "gives the film its soul." The final moments, as Jack captures his perfect scream, offer a heart-wrenching glimpse into a tortured soul that De Palma has never quite matched.

Scarface (1983)

"CUBANS! COCAINE! AL PACINO! MACHINE GUNS! GIRLS! WOW! That's what I want to see," De Palma told 'Esquire' on the set of what began life as a straight remake of Howard Hawks' 1932 underworld classic of the same name. Delivering on his promise, De Palma thrust the ultra-violence of his *Scarface* into the Florida sunshine, far from the concealed depictions of aggression in vintage film noir.

Cut to a blood-soaked bathroom in an art deco apartment on Ocean Drive, Miami Beach. The director looks on as Tony Montana (Al Pacino) is forced, at gunpoint, to watch as his brother Angel (Pepe Serna) has his leg cut off with a chainsaw during a botched drug deal with a Colombian drug cartel. Angel's severed arm is already hanging, handcuffed, to the

shower rail. Such cold-blooded excess surges through *Scarface*, a loaded-gun project of volatile components that went on to transform De Palma's stock - and the gangster genre.

But beyond such modern divergences from Hawks' original, what sent this '80s paean to maniacal corruption into cult folklore is Montana, a power-mad immigrant living the American dream. He became an anti-hero pin-up. Audiences were attracted to Pacino's incredible embodiment of psychotic greed. While Montana was, categorically, the bad guy - his downfall inevitable, never glorified - the unrepentant drug baron became a pop-culture icon, more than any Scorsese mobster. De Palma scored his most successful film to date, even though it was hardly an obvious fit for him. In hindsight, fusing De Palma's suspense-ridden bravura set-pieces with the epic tale of a criminal life spiralling out of control is perfect. The brainchild of *Serpico* producer Martin Bregman, *Scarface* came to De Palma while he was shooting *Blow Out*. He turned it down, due to having his hands full, and Sidney Lumet was briefly attached. When Lumet walked out over script conflicts, De Palma - bruised by the response to *Blow Out* and desperate to leave his latest assignment *Flashdance* - signed on. Scripted by Oliver Stone - yet to make a name as a director, but still hot after his 1978 Oscar win for his *Midnight Express* screenplay - *Scarface*'s action was moved to the hot, sweaty climes of Miami during the Mariel boatlift in 1980 (when Cuban refugees were given free entry to the States).

The rest is revisionist history. The political backdrop may have thrilled Stone and De Palma, but it also caused major problems. No sooner had the cameras rolled on *Scarface* than protests started. Despite having not read the script, the local Cuban community was incensed at its portrayal as cocaine-dealing, trigger-happy criminals. While *Scarface* is Pacino's film, the ensemble playing Montana's extended criminal family is also superb. Michelle Pfeiffer (fresh from *Grease 2*) plays Elvira Hancock, the object of Montana's affection and moll to his boss, Frank Lopez (Robert Loggia). Stephen Bauer and Mary Elizabeth Mastrantonio, as Montana's long-suffering friend Manny and sister Gina respectively, also excel.

Montana's rise and fall, including a delightfully '80s cash-counting montage, is a brutal and violent tragedy that takes no prisoners. Violence was something De Palma knew all too well. Often admonished for his penchant for on-screen butchery, nothing could have prepared the director for his duel with the American censors. The board rated *Scarface* as 'X'. Not a big surprise when the F-bomb is dropped 226 times. The aforementioned chainsaw battle - vaunted by Tarantino as the precursor to the infamous ear scene in *Reservoir Dogs* (1992) - and copious drug use (including Montana face down in a mountain of cocaine), wouldn't have helped the film's cause either. De Palma had to go into negotiation overdrive to secure an 'R'-rating. When the film premiered on December 1, 1983, in New York City, including a disclaimer to placate Miami's Cuban community, the response was mixed. Reviews focused on the bloodletting and profanity. Even New York film critic Kael, normally De Palma's staunchest supporter, knocked it as "a sloppy piece of movie-making."

Time has been kinder to De Palma's cult classic. The garish fashions, outrageous dialogue and extreme bloodletting constantly bring *Scarface* to new followers. While dozens of pretenders have tried to appropriate *Scarface*'s shocking portrayal of the criminal underworld, few come close to matching it. There will only ever be one Tony Montana. "Say goodbye to the bad guy."

Body Double (1984)

Ever the spoilt (movie) brat, De Palma was not a happy camper when *Scarface* caused a furore with US censors. In a petulant move, he announced that his next film would be a salacious 'X'-rated hardcore shocker featuring unsimulated sex. That would show 'em. 'American Psycho' Patrick Bateman's favourite film, *Body Double*, was the result.

While this racy mix of Hitchcockian tropes - inspired by the body double for Angie Dickinson's shower scene in *Dressed to Kill* - certainly doesn't penetrate the porn world as originally intended, the LA story of down-on-his-luck actor Jake (Craig Wasson) being set up to witness a murder certainly has enough ribald dialogue (mainly from Melanie Griffith's perky porn star Holly Body), copious nudity and gratuitous phallic drill violence to make it the guiltiest of pleasures.

But only just. Alas, it also has a horrendous performance by then-hot *Dallas* star Deborah Shelton as the object of Jake's desire, a fatally guessable plot and a bizarre

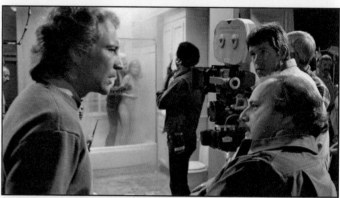

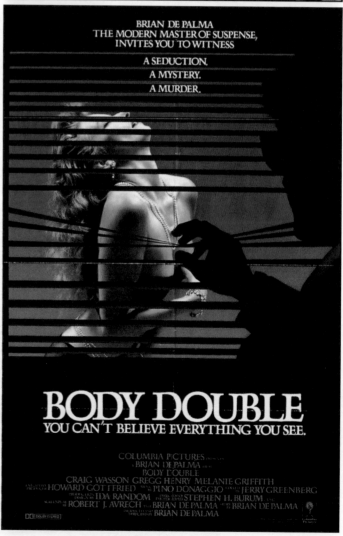

BRIAN DE PALMA
THE MODERN MASTER OF SUSPENSE,
INVITES YOU TO WITNESS

A SEDUCTION.
A MYSTERY.
A MURDER.

BODY DOUBLE
YOU CAN'T BELIEVE EVERYTHING YOU SEE.

COLUMBIA PICTURES
BRIAN DE PALMA
BODY DOUBLE
CRAIG WASSON GREGG HENRY MELANIE GRIFFITH
HOWARD GOTTFRIED PINO DONAGGIO JERRY GREENBERG
IDA RANDOM STEPHEN H. BURUM
ROBERT J. AVRECH BRIAN DE PALMA BRIAN DE PALMA
BRIAN DE PALMA

appearance from pop band Frankie Goes to Hollywood performing *Relax*.

It was Griffith who came out of the film unscathed. The role of Holly was given to Annette Haven before Columbia bulked at casting a real-life porn star. Tatum O'Neal, Jamie Lee Curtis and Carrie Fisher all auditioned for the role and Brooke Shields and Linda Hamilton both turned it down. Griffith gives a knowing and frank performance that led to her star turns in *Something Wild* (1986) and *Working Girl* (1988). The film also marked the fifth and final time that De Palma worked with Dennis Franz after *The Fury*, *Dressed to Kill*, *Blow Out* and *Scarface*.

Body Double is the director's love letter to the artificiality of '80s Los Angeles. Full of landmarks - including Tail o' the Pup, the Beverly Center, Barney's Beanery, the LA Farmer's Market, the Rodeo Collection mall on Rodeo Drive and Chemosphere House off Mulholland Drive from where Jake first witnesses, through a telescope, the erotic dance that draws him into the dark side of Hollywood - De Palma's voyeuristic sun-bleached neo-noir is as audacious as it is crass. Despite the technical brilliance on display, from De Palma's trademark technical trickery to Stephen H. Burum's dreamlike photography and Donaggio's lush romantic score, *Body Double*'s proclivity for misogynistic violence ensure that this garish murder mystery remains the director's most divisive film. Where Roger Ebert called *Body Double* an "exhilarating exercise in pure filmmaking", many critics were far less kind. "*Body Double* was reviled when it came out," De Palma told 'The Guardian' in 2016. "It really hurt. I got slaughtered by the press right at the height of the women's liberation movement... I thought it was completely unjustified. It was a suspense thriller, and I was always interested in finding new ways to kill people."

Wise Guys (1986)

The backlash against *Scarface and Body Double* saw De Palma retreating to a genre he hadn't visited since his early days doing experimental comedies like *Murder a La Mod* (1968), *Greetings* (1968) and *Hi, Mom!* (1970). After a disastrous experience filming *Get to Know Your Rabbit* (1972) with Orson Welles, De Palma had rarely attempted to tickle the funny bone. Yes, his horror-tinged pop pastiche *Phantom of the Paradise* (1974) delighted in skewering the music industry to hilarious effect and many of his subsequent thrillers made sly digs at the genre, but no-one really came to a De Palma movie in search of laughs.

Unfortunately, *Wise Guys* still left audiences wanting in the laughter department. Despite a cast boasting Danny DeVito, Joe Piscopo, Dan Hedaya and Harvey Keitel, plus a return to the genre that made *Scarface* so memorable, *Wise Guys* fails on almost every level.

In a decade that saw De Palma say no to *Flashdance* (1983) and *Fatal Attraction* (1987), both eventually shot by Adrian Lyne, it's difficult to see what compelled him to say yes to this.

The usually reliable DeVito and Piscopo play Harry Valentini and Moe Dickstein, two hapless errand boys for Newark Mafia boss Anthony Castelo (Hedaya). They usually spend their time doing the jobs no-one else wants, like looking after their mob boss's goldfish, testing out bullet-proof jackets or checking the boss's car for bombs. That is until they

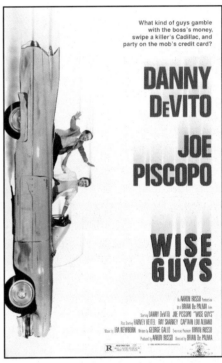

inadvertently lose $250,000 of Castelo's money during a botched bet on a rigged horse race. They are set up to kill each other but instead, they run off to Atlantic City. Hilarity does not ensue.

It's telling that the music video De Palma shot a couple of years earlier, for Bruce Springsteen's *Dancing in the Dark* from his globe-conquering *Born in the USA* album, is more fondly remembered than this blank-firing gangster comedy. Luckily De Palma was able to quickly wipe this comic misfire from our memories with his next film, The Untouchables. As De Palma told the 'Business Insider': "Now, a movie I wish I hadn't done was *Wise Guys*. The studio changed its minds and didn't want to make it. They just wanted us to go away. I should have just taken my money and walked instead of dealing with a studio that didn't want to make the movie."

The Untouchables (1987)

After the double box-office failures of *Body Double* and *Wise Guys*, De Palma was in desperate need of a hit. *The Untouchables*, written by David Mamet, the talented scribe behind *The Postman Always Rings Twice* (1981), *The Verdict* (1982) and *Glengarry Glen Ross* (1992), and based on the book of the same name that inspired the hit '50s

television show starring Robert Stack as Eliot Ness, was the crowd-pleaser that finally introduced De Palma to a movie mainstream that would later see him directing Tom Cruise in *Mission: Impossible* (1996).

The epic gangster drama introduced the world to Kevin Costner, reunited De Palma with Robert de Niro and gave Sean Connery a Best Supporting Actor Oscar-winning role. Set in a beautifully captured Prohibition-era Chicago, Costner takes on the role of a clean-cut Eliot Ness, the Bureau of Prohibition agent trying to bring down Al Capone (De Niro). Connery, along with Andy Garcia and

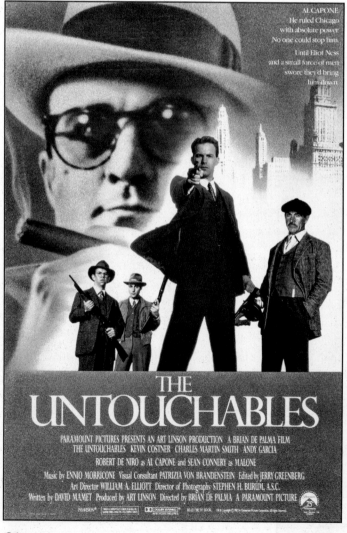

86

Charles Martin Smith, play the police officers who Ness recruits to join his 'untouchable' squad.

De Niro put on weight for the role of the notorious gangster Al Capone and wore silk underwear, like Capone, to get into character. Despite having helped introduce De Niro to the movie-going public, De Palma still had to wine and dine his friend for the role as he explained to Noah Baumbach and Jake Paltrow in their brilliant documentary *De Palma* (2015): "Bobby takes a long time to decide to do things. You go out to dinner with him, you talk about the script, and it took many, many weeks until he finally said: 'Yeah, I think that we can make this work.'"

"I had trouble with some of the scenes with [De Niro]," Costner explained to 'Entertainment Weekly' when talking about keeping such illustrious company. "Because my character was very straight-arrow, and Robert was able to jump off the page. I was trying to survive with my straight-arrow language against someone who was throwing a level of street language at me that had a level of improv to it. So, it was hard for me to survive in some of those scenes, and Sean [Connery] talked to me a little bit about it."

It's Connery, as the irascible veteran Irish-American beat cop Jimmy Malone, who won the biggest accolades, despite his unfaltering Scottish accent. Only De Niro's ominous 'enthusiasms' monologue, that ends with the gangster caving-in a fellow criminal's head with a baseball bat, threatens to match Connery's scene-stealing performance.

Beautifully shot by *Body Double* cinematographer Burum with lavish period detail and a sublime, uplifting score by Ennio Morricone, *The Untouchables* even gives De Palma a western moment as Ness and his 'untouchables' ride on horseback, guns blazing, to stop a liquor shipment at the Canadian Border.

It's the Union Station shootout, however, for which *The Untouchables* is justly renowned. Channelling the Odessa Steps scene in Sergei Eisenstein's 1925 propaganda film *Battleship Potemkin*, the sequence sees Ness and George Stone (Garcia) caught in a blazing gun battle involving gangsters, innocent passers-by and an oblivious baby in a pram rolling down the station's central stairs in heart-stopping slow-motion. It's a masterful piece of filmmaking that plays out in excruciating real-time as the agents wait for their quarry, Al Capone's head bookkeeper, to arrive. The resulting firefight is an exhilarating pay-off that proves there is no one better than De Palma at cranking up the tension to breaking point.

Casualties of War (1989)

By the time he took the lead in De Palma's savage Vietnam condemnation, Michael J. Fox was one of the biggest names in the world. With *Teen Wolf* (1985) and *Back to the Future* (1985), the beloved *Family Ties* actor had made

IT'S NOT THE ENEMY
YOU FIGHT TO KILL,
BUT THE INNOCENT YOU FAIL
TO SAVE.

Casualties of War

the leap from television star to Hollywood hero. With roles in Herbert Ross' *The Secret of My Success* (1987) and James Bridges' *Bright Lights, Big City* (1988), he was growing up in public.

Hailed by Quentin Tarantino as "the greatest film about the Vietnam War", *Casualties of War* proved what a great actor Fox could be. We knew that he had charisma to spare as he more than proved on the Robert Zemeckis time-travelling adventure, but with De Palma's brutal indictment of American soldiers during the endless war that nobody wanted, the diminutive actor holds his own against a stunning ensemble.

The film is based on an article written by Daniel Lang for the 'New Yorker' in 1969, which chronicled events of the 1966 incident on Hill 192 during the Vietnam War, in which a young Vietnamese woman was kidnapped from her village by a squad of American soldiers and raped and murdered by them. The screenplay was written by *The Firm* (1993) scribe David Rabe who later disassociated himself from the film, saying that De Palma had not been faithful to his script.

"*Casualties of War* took, I don't know, a decade to get made," the director told Matt Zoller Seitz on RogerEbert. com. "I read the story in the '60s and was later given the option to develop it. And it was only after the success of *The Untouchables* that I was finally able to get control of the property."

De Palma cast Fox as Erickson because he embodied an American innocent and had an integrity to everything that he did. He plays the only member of his platoon with any kind of moral compass. The rest are played by Sean Penn, John C. Reilly, John Leguizamo and Don Patrick Harvey. Penn, who would again work with De Palma in *Carlito's Way* (1993), is astonishing as Sergeant Tony Meserve, the instigator of the atrocity which leaves conscientious objector Erickson ostracized by his fellow soldiers.

Full of intense set pieces - especially the death of bloody and bruised victim Tran Thi Oanh (Thuy Thu Le) as she tries to escape her captors on the railroad bridge during an intense

gun battle, some typically De Palma-esque tracking shots as the soldiers walk through the beautifully shot locations in Thailand, and a wonderous score by maestro Morricone - *Casualties of War* shows De Palma handling an atypical genre, for him, with aplomb.

By taking the cliches of the war movie and spinning the expected machismo on its head, De Palma comments not only about the war and the terrible deeds done in the name of victory, but also on his own films, often criticised for victimising and ghettoising women. He, himself, said of his testosterone-fuelled films of the latter part of the decade: "They're gangster movies; they're war movies! Movies like that tend to be very masculine." But with Michael J. Fox, he found a hero who was the very antithesis of those gung-ho heroics.

Ending the decade with a bang, the beginning of the '90s saw the director lauded for his films in the '80s but chastised for attempting to adapt Tom Wolfe's seminal tome 'The Bonfire of the Vanities' in 1990. His big budget folly saw him reuniting him with his *Body Double* star Griffith but was hamstrung by fatally miscast performances by Bruce Willis and Tom Hanks. Much like the beginning of the '80s, the high-profile failure saw the director retreating to the genres in which he had made his name with *Raising Cain* (1992) and *Carlito's Way* (1993). Whatever the director did from that point forth, looking back, the '80s was his decade.

Cruising: Outcry!

by Aaron Stielstra

Enough has been revisited or resurrected about William Friedkin's disturbing 1980 film *Cruising* to make for a lot of fabricated and redundant content. There's an enormous amount of supplementary material available on Blu-rays and the internet, for example. While watching the movie, viewers are likely to be distracted by their own expectations born from their familiarity with the cop .vs. killer sub-genre. They may end up focusing on the graphic shocks, the 'did-they-film-that-or-not' trivia, or the depiction of the S&M leather scene itself.

What many viewers are likely to overlook is the fact that Friedkin's compelling suspense movie is a work of surreal art, a mystery that appears to investigate murders but, more than that, takes its audience on a challenging ride. It's a gripping urban story which still qualifies as a cop thriller but uses a film grammar all its own, showing an unapologetic approach to storytelling.

This unusual style was the result of dire production conditions during shooting. It was while remedying the technical damage to his film (mostly caused by rabid gay rights protesters who committed visual and audio sabotage during the NYC shoot in the summer of 1979) that Friedkin found something unique.

When I met the actor Don Scardino, who plays Ted in the film, he described to me how the protesters regularly hijacked filming in the Village by using whistles, bullhorns and mirrors. Oftentimes, Al Pacino had to be rushed on and off the set in a police car for his own safety. It is hard to think of any thriller made nowadays - let alone a 'straight' movie - capable of arousing such an outcry. This production hell gave birth to an injured product, but Friedkin dove headfirst into the rescue effort and produced a highly original abstract thriller.

The genesis of Friedkin's radical movie began with author Gerald Walker's misanthropic 1970 novel. The narrative and dialogue remain mostly intact from the book, yet the environs and the character wardrobes are more in tune with Friedkin's earlier *The Boys in the Band* (1970). Unlike the screen version's bomber caps and leather boots, the book offers fruity-coloured shirts and sandals! The kind of optimistic cruising gear described in the book would get you denied entry to the Mineshaft any night of the week! The book's pickup scene is more like something from *Advise & Consent* (1962), though the patrons in Otto Preminger's film were less confined to a single Stonewall-type bar - they wandered the streets and enjoyed their own cruising neighbourhoods.

The gay bars themselves, where Detective Steve Burns unhappily lingers in wait for the killer, reflect the novel's time period. The book summons images of the kind of 'hippie-queers' who populated Gordon Douglas' *The Detective* (1968) or Don Siegel's *Coogan's Bluff* (1968), dancing to fuzz-tone guitar and tambourines. The West Village, the meatpacking district and the Chelsea piers in the film are replaced by classier dives on the Upper West side.

Though real-life NYC police detective Randy Jurgensen's undercover investigation into a slew of homosexual murders influenced Friedkin's screenplay, the novel contributes most of the plot and the characters found in the movie. The Jurgensen material, though factual, is here turned upside-down and establishes the central ambiguity between the cop and his prey. This is complemented by Friedkin's bizarro interpretation of what happens when a detective goes too deep undercover.

If another director were to approach the adaptation, a Godforsaken voice-over (or two) might accompany. Yet both narrators in the book are unbalanced. The character motivations - and in the killer's case, a terrifying, shrieking schizophrenia - offer minimal explanation. As portrayed by Pacino in the screen version, Detective Steve Burns makes cryptic comments like, "There's a lot about me you don't know about", and, "I guess you can't be too careful", yet his remarks are met with silence or incomprehension by his fellows.

The bar scenes are more characterised in the film. The bars themselves become secondary characters, with Friedkin really going to town by providing a stylised, graphic travelogue of gathering spots that appear like sweaty, shifting chambers of Hades. The fetishistic costumes are colourful and their environments even more unnerving. There are flashes of dark humour too, such as when Pacino faces a disappointed bouncer on why his attire doesn't match the establishment's 'Precinct Night' dress code of cop uniforms. Later, laconic salesman Powers Boothe explains the coded identities behind different coloured pocket hankies, a variety that covers everything from oral sex to golden showers. Boothe delivers his salesman pitch as if he's selling hard drives!

The bar scenes are shot in surreal fashion, using jump cuts, flash cuts, recycled shots, slow-motion and other visual manoeuvres reminiscent of Nicolas Roeg, or Godard, or Hal Ashby's editorial work in *The Loved One* (1965). Additionally, a slew of musclebound, athletic rock 'n' roll accompanies the montages at full volume. More on the soundtrack later.

The most effective of Friedkin's manipulations is his sound design. Here, the director's penchant for

imaginative audio shocks is on par with his work in *The Exorcist* (1973). The menacing killer's voice is not a belching, demonic Regan incantating, "You made me do that". Instead, it suggests a building psychosis that could turn supernatural. The audio superimpositions extend to music, sometimes numbering as high as three tracks at once, blending different pieces of melodies.

Using animal squeals and other gut-thumping, visceral embellishments, Friedkin also uses the killer's voice multiple times in the post-dubbing work. The voice travels between different suspects, including a flashback character. This likely distracted (or frightened) the movie's numerous critics. The effect is one of disorientation. Spaghetti westerns create an otherworldly feel to the faces onscreen with their disembodied and intimately recorded voices. This claustrophobic lack of space is further increased here in a movie that offers its characters very little space.

If the protestors knew that dubbing repairs would lead to the kind of sound heard in the first murder sequence, maybe they would have allowed the sound as originally recorded. Here, the victim's swallows and killer's whispers are so intimate, it seems the microphones are placed surgically. Thus, the violence is maximised and pretty

agonising to watch. The procedural scenes involving cops, undercover stings and other gritty NYC confrontations between diverse characters like Joe Spinell's damaged cop or Gene Davis' wisecracking cross-dressing prostitute are still strong in the movie. Yet the murder and characterisation scenes, with their tampered vocals and unsettling style, are a departure from, say, a Sidney Lumet thriller. Considering serial killer movies hadn't reached their zenith in the '80s (and serial killers wouldn't achieve their unwelcome rock-star status until the '90s onwards), the unique 'going-into-the-killer's-POV' was limited to Hitchcock or Michael Powell's *Peeping Tom*. TV-movies usually stuck to the facts about Son of Sam or other murderers and their madness, be they feature length or mini-series like *The Atlanta Child Murders* (1985).

Here, unlike Michael Mann's sleek *Manhunter* (1986), the duality of the cop/killer is one jagged ride - and a daunting relationship for fans of generic, diluted thrillers to absorb. It was obviously a challenge for a 1980 audience to watch a story with a cop protagonist told in a such a non-linear manner.

To add to all this chaos, the *Cruising* soundtrack is a masterwork, a memorable combination of offbeat artists. Friedkin's research into the bar scene music revealed

that patrons - mostly dressed as macho bikers, military types and cops - liked to dance to Donna Summer and Abba in bars with names like the The Ambush and The Spike. Friedkin's soundtrack creates a properly menacing landscape far removed from what you might hear on a Bee Gees album, and it's hard to imagine the walls of the movie's numerous grimily authentic locales throbbing with the *Thank God it's Friday* (1978) soundtrack. What would those neglected disco artists have thought if their hits appeared in Friedkin's movie, serenading chained-up, harnessed sex slaves and amyl-nitrate-popping cowboys?

Friedkin opts instead to use the likes of the Cripples, Willy DeVille, Rough Trade and the Germs mixed with the complex Jack Nitzsche score which combines synthesizer, percussion and ominous Spanish guitar, the latter two elements arriving at the killer's introduction. The minimalist melodies and patterns are stunning. They sustain a whole new atmosphere that is as exciting as it is strange.

The mix of punk and funk - like the exceptional *Lump* by Mutiny - is hard to ignore, as the songs inspire endless cruisers to bounce around onscreen. If it doesn't create some gay underworld subtext, it does at least show that gay-bar DJs in the *Cruising* universe had great musical taste.

Other than turning the mystery-cop genre on its head, the movie invited more attacks, and not just from the gay rights protesters and the uninformed. These attacks stemmed from the movie's ambiguity and there was a lot of easily sparked, empty criticism from those who rejected *Cruising* as being unworthy of controversy. They called it something worse: "a clumsy, muddled thriller."

Friedkin featured ambiguity in his other films, including *Sorcerer* (1977) or the ominous final gunshot in *The French Connection* (1971). Walker's novel features the same bleak climax, though the events play out more savagely. Whatever the reason(s) for mainstream audiences rejecting *Cruising* (the graphic sex, violence or nihilism are acceptable enough criteria), its ambiguous conclusion seemed the most unforgivable. After watching a movie play with such extreme styles while offering Mondo-exploitative-anthropological shocks in its explicit bar scenes - plus songs like *Spy Boy* by John Hiatt - did people really expect a square ending to this thriller? A movie where music is often played backwards? It's ugly, unseemly and fascinating but it doesn't pander. It refuses to supply anything as unbelievable (or insulting) as a bogus Hollywood ending.

Friedkin delivered plenty of tough drama and thrills and realism in other movies and he does so here. The visceral, strange horror dressed in a cop film package comes with a price - you don't get a neat wrap-up to Pacino's ordeal. Maybe if Friedkin had gone with his original idea of casting a young Richard Gere as Detective Steve Burns, the character's transformation would have been more believable than seeing impressionable 40-year-old Pacino inexplicably turning into a monster, burdened with a terrible perm and an anaemic green pallor.

Nonetheless, it's hard to imagine any conclusion to either Walker's book or Friedkin's movie that offers a sense of hope. By sticking to being a modern urban-horror story about a forbidden, subterranean world of rough sex, the film's opening disclaimer card, sanctioned by United Artists and the MPAA, is absurd. It declares the film "is not intended as an indictment of the homosexual world. It is set in one small segment of that world." Is this supposed to justify or rationalize Friedkin's intriguing, loopy narrative, as if we were about to watch a documentary instead of fiction? Like Friedkin stated: "the characters were never meant to be emblematic."

Maybe its purpose was to clarify that 'mainstream' gays don't appear in the film. Yet, putting aside the fact that most of the bar extras were willing participants, just who exactly is this 'small segment' of New York City presented in *Cruising*? With the story so unusually told, due to Friedkin's mad-scientist editing and sound design, would it not be more logical to say these characters simply exist in a dark, debauched world where the phantom of AIDS looms over the horizon as deadly as the movie's killer?

But as an abstract purgatory of a narrative, told on its own disturbing terms and orchestrated by a director who was out to discompose as well as entertain, the movie works. It succeeds in creating a world scarier than those captured in killer-on-the-loose fare like the same year's *The First Deadly Sin*, or an exploitation piece like *Maniac*.

Not many viewers cared to visit the world depicted in *Cruising* in 1980. Or maybe, with good reason, they were too scared.

AL PACINO IS CRUISING FOR A KILLER.

A WILLIAM FRIEDKIN FILM

CRUISING

LORIMAR PRESENTS A JERRY WEINTRAUB PRODUCTION
AL PACINO WILLIAM FRIEDKIN'S "CRUISING"
PAUL SORVINO KAREN ALLEN PRODUCED BY JERRY WEINTRAUB
WRITTEN FOR THE SCREEN AND DIRECTED BY WILLIAM FRIEDKIN
BASED UPON THE NOVEL BY GERALD WALKER MUSIC JACK NITZSCHE TECHNICOLOR
ORIGINAL SOUNDTRACK ALBUM ON LORIMAR RECORDS · SILVER FEROX DESIGN

CRAVEN IMAGES
Inside The Serpent and the Rainbow

Brian J. Robb explores the troubled making of Wes Craven's *The Serpent and the Rainbow*.

Following the disappointment of the poorly received *Deadly Friend* (1986), writer-director Wes Craven entered a new creative phase during which he produced three of his most accomplished works: *The Serpent and the Rainbow* (1988), *Shocker* (1989) and *The People Under the Stairs* (1991). Finally, aged 49, he had enough power in the film industry to exert control over his projects. Determined to broaden his genre horizons beyond horror, Craven was looking for a project which would rise above the run-of-the-mill fright flicks he was being offered. "For a long time, I'd been looking for a crossover piece that would use the benefits and momentum of my reputation as a horror director to get me into more of an adult venue."

Executive producer Rob Cohen felt he had a project perfect for Craven. Producers David Ladd (son of actor Alan Ladd) and Doug Claybourne had bought the film rights to a recently published non-fiction book called 'The Serpent and the Rainbow', about the true-life experiences of an anthropologist in Haiti. Reading the book, Craven discovered a fascinating true story which followed up many of the concepts he had been exploring, including altered states of consciousness and the boundaries between nightmares and the waking world. "Once I'd read the book, I signed on right away without seeing the script.

I knew that anything made from it would be wonderful. Wade Davis was approached by a pharmaceutical firm and a financier and was given the assignment to go into Haiti and try to penetrate the voodoo cults and find out whether there was any truth to the rumours about zombies. They were thought to be mythological, but they were actually people that had been poisoned by a drug that made them appear to be dead. Davis had this incredible adventure, meeting a magician in the interior of Haiti who makes these powders."

Richard Maxwell had the job of writing a script from the often dry and scientific prose of Davis' true-life account of his adventure in 1982 in pre-revolutionary Haiti. Davis was searching for the drug which induced the zombie state, with the aim of bringing it back to the United States for use in medicine. The inevitable dream sequences were added by Craven after Maxwell had left the project. "I had the entire climax of the film done as a nightmare under the influence of the drug in order to rationalise what the previous screenwriter had left me with. I felt that the film being about voodoo and the research into voodoo and how much we found that it influences the interior of the mind, there could be a great deal of dreams and hallucination. It's an organic, natural part of it. It was actually very powerful to expand the film in that way."

There was also a political dimension, which allowed Craven to make a more adult movie than he'd done in recent years. "In the 1970s and 1980s, voodoo had been corrupted by Duvalier [Haiti's then dictator] and used for political terrorism. So the film was about that adventure of Wade Davis [Bill Pullman played the Davis equivalent, Dennis Alan] and it had this very strong political element in the confrontation with the Ton Ton Macoute [Haitian secret police]. It also had the love story between Pullman and Cathy Tyson. Wade Davis was guided on his search by a beautiful young Haitian woman, and they did fall in love, so major elements of the movie parallel Wade Davis' life."

This was to be a commercial film that needed elements of adventure, romance, politics and conflict, all of which could be drawn naturally from the source material. There was one thing missing: Craven's archetypal strong villain. "We created an antagonist for the Davis character to go up against. The villain is the symbol for all the terrorism in the country, and Alan takes it upon himself to get rid of him. Essentially, it's still Davis' story of looking for the zombie drug. All the elements of voodoo, zombies and Haiti's exotic mystery were so good, it would have been a mistake to mess with them. Wade Davis was pretty happy - he understood we were making a commercial picture."

In keeping with Craven's desire to broaden his range, he aimed to make a much more rounded film than he'd done before. "It was my first movie out of the genre in the sense that it had a love story and politics and a big budget of $11 million. It had big crowds, 4,000 people in one scene. On the other hand, when the whole third act takes place within a hallucination of the main character when he's poisoned by this substance and we go inside his mind, it's pure Wes Craven stuff." Producer David Ladd agreed that *The Serpent and the Rainbow* was more involved than Craven's previous supernatural outings. "There is a difference," noted Ladd. "Horror films owe nothing to truth, while stories of terror stem from some aspect of reality, as this one does."

The Serpent and the Rainbow was also the first film to take Craven out of the United States. "It was a very important film for me in the sense that it gave me the chance to expand my palette and shoot on actual locations in Haiti. It was quite an intensive piece to shoot, working with full-blooded voodoo people. We were working within a very narrow window between two revolutions in Haiti, where things were very unstable." Craven took his first trip to Haiti late in 1986 in the company of Ladd, to scout possible locations and to make themselves known to the powerful local politicians and voodoo witch doctors. It was the beginning of a terrifying experience which made Craven's *Nightmare on Elm Street* films look like pleasant dreams.

Awakened in the middle of the night by their voodoo

hosts, Craven and Ladd were taken to a field where a party was in progress. As he got used to his surroundings - the music, the drinking, the dancing - it dawned on Craven that this was a voodoo ceremony. A pig was suddenly produced and slaughtered about five feet away from the startled director. The gathered throng began screaming and the blood from the pig was collected in buckets and circulated to be drunk. As the bucket drew closer, Craven grew paler. The priest in charge did not make his Hollywood guests drink, which came as a huge relief to Craven. "We were lucky, because, based on what we had already learned about voodoo, you can be in serious trouble if you don't drink it." The pig incident didn't alter Craven's plans to shoot at least part of the film on location in Haiti, the first American feature film to do so. "Originally, we were going to shoot it in Mexico, but when we went to Haiti to scout, we discovered it had so much potential. It's got great scenery and presence, and we were able to get hundreds of extras really cheaply."

Casting proved problematic. The subject matter of voodoo and zombies put many actors off, with names such as Kyle MacLachlan, Kevin Bacon and even Al Pacino turning Craven down. Finally, he found Bill Pullman, who was best known for his comedic role as Captain Lonestar in Mel Brooks' *Star Wars* spoof *Spaceballs*. "We were lucky to get Bill Pullman," noted Craven, "and he was pleased to have a role which showed what he could do; there's Indiana Jones style adventuring, love scenes, good hero stuff." Pullman became an under-rated leading man, with his appearances as the US President in *Independence Day* and its sequel, and as a moody jazz saxophonist in David Lynch's bizarre and brutal *Lost Highway*. It would be Pullman's job to pull off the emotional and physical exertions Craven would put *The Serpent and the Rainbow*'s hero through.

The other roles were slightly easier to fill, and many of Craven's first choices fell into place. "I go for villains to be as nasty as they can be and Zakes Mokae had no problem with it. I had some criticism about that: the white hero and the black villain, but it's about a black religion, a black country, black culture. There's the Paul Winfield character, who's very intelligent, political and powerful. And there's Cathy Tyson, who's independent and the love interest. We had some trouble in the southern states because of the love scenes between the white guy and the black girl."

Craven arrived back in Haiti with his cast and crew in late February to prepare for the beginning of principal photography on 9 March 1987. The first thing the director did was arrange a blessing for the movie from the local voodoo 'bokor', a witch doctor. Protection from evil spirits was granted and Craven set out to film for 30 days in Haiti's grim, unhealthy slums and cemeteries. A rough shoot was expected, but nothing like the problems they actually faced. Almost all the cast and crew were ill by

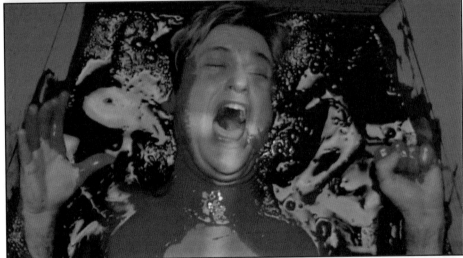

the second day. The sickness - manifest in the form of nausea, vomiting or dizziness - persisted throughout the location shoot, but Craven himself escaped. "I felt protected," he declared, "and was determined not to be invaded by what was going on."

Illness was not the only spectre stalking the production. Tales abound of crew members so affected by the voodoo atmosphere that they were unable to work. Incidents of hallucinations among the crew were legion, some more serious than others. "People were having wild hallucinations," said Craven. "One person went completely mad after talking to a magician and had to be shipped back to the United States. He snapped out of it five days later. Very strange events were happening all the time, so it was quite an adventure to make."

Strange occurrences dogged the production throughout early March 1987. Bill Pullman was not immune to the fear and unease spreading through the cast and crew and claimed to have seen a green cow with television screens for eyes. Another crew member was convinced he had seen a long dead general on horseback. The general had approached and pleaded with him to give him the colour blue!

Every morning the cast and crew awoke to another oppressive Haitian day and made their way through the streets, which ran with raw sewage in ditches, to that day's location. Craven had secured the co-operation of the Haitian government and the Department of Culture, so the crew were under the protection of the local militia and a village police station served as the payroll base for the employment of thousands of locals as extras.

Throughout shooting, the political tensions on the island increased. Craven decided it was time to call a halt as things were becoming too risky to remain in Haiti. "We left the country the next day. It became apparent that the place was a time bomb, so we had to get out. All of us came away feeling very much attached to Haiti..." As the crew finished the last scheduled scene at the airport, they took the opportunity to hop on a plane that was being used as a prop and leave the turbulent island behind, relocating to the comparatively safer conditions of the Dominican Republic for the remaining eight weeks of production, where filming finally wrapped on 12 May, 1987.

Craven was gratified by the favourable response to the movie at several test screenings, and *The Serpent and the Rainbow* was released in the United States on 15 January, 1988. "It was very well received critically, did well at the box office and won Best Film, Best Director and Best Screenplay at the Madrid Film Festival. It was also a big hit in Japan," he recalled. In the US alone, the film grossed just under $20 million.

For the critics, *The Serpent and the Rainbow* was simultaneously both a mature departure from Craven's past formulaic horrors and yet another example of more of the same old horror stuff. "Offers a few good scares, but gets bogged down in special effects," was the blunt assessment in 'Variety'. 'Time Out' stated: "Unfortunately, the political parallel between the ideological repression of [the] regime and the stultifying effects of the zombifying fluid is only sketchily developed, leaving us with a series of striking but isolated set pieces." As far as Richard Harrington in the 'Washington Post' was concerned, Craven had taken "a powerful, revealing non-fiction book" and "sifted through it for its most cliched elements, turning it into a terror film."

As so often before, critic Roger Ebert rode to Craven's defence. "*The Serpent and the Rainbow* is uncanny in the way it takes the most lurid images and makes them plausible." In his new movie, according to Desson Thompson, also writing in the 'Washington Post': "[Craven] seems wiser and more story-conscious, but thankfully still full of the same surprises." Jonathan Rosenbaum, writing in the 'Chicago Reader', tackled Craven's *The Serpent and the Rainbow* as seriously as Craven intended the film to be received. "An unusually ambitious effort from horror movie specialist Wes Craven... this [is a] genuinely frightening thriller. Depending largely on hallucinations and psychological terror, Craven provides more atmosphere and creepy ideas than fluid storytelling. It's nice to see some of the virtues of old-fashioned horror films, moody dream sequences, unsettling poetic images, and passages that suggest more than they show rather than the usual splatter shocks."

With the success of *The Serpent and the Rainbow*, Craven realised that he had the ability to combine his aptitude for horror with more mainstream themes or subjects and turn out good movies. "I had to do something I had never anticipated - I had to come to terms with the fact that I do have a capacity to generate horror films, horror images. Somehow those images from our own culture affect me profoundly and I'm able to put them onto film. There is

an element that I enjoy that I denied for many years. I'm trying now to be more mature about it and say that I have to admit that there is a part of me that is this wild maniac, that loves these crazy images, that loves to scare people and enjoys going into these very dark labyrinths of human consciousness. I must not try to deny that outlet. I feel I can do that very well, and I feel that I can do a lot of other things well, so the trick is not to just kick it out of my life but to make room for the other things as well."

Making *The Serpent and the Rainbow* changed Craven in a way that no other filmmaking experience would. "Haiti really mellowed me out. I almost died down there, and I experienced a lot of strange things. So, when I came through it all, not only alive, but healthy, I decided to begin taking my life a bit easier. The experience was definitely therapeutic. I've learned about another place and I've learned much about myself."

Brian J. Robb's 'Screams & Nightmares: The Films of Wes Craven' (Polaris Books) is available now in a fully revised and updated hardback edition from bookshops and online.

CLOSING CREDITS

Simon J. Ballard
Simon lives in Oxford and works in its oldest building, a Saxon Tower. Whilst also working in the adjoining church, he has never felt tempted to re-enact scenes from *Taste the Blood of Dracula* or *Dracula A.D.1972*. He has never done this. Ever. He regularly contributes to the magazine 'We Belong Dead' and its various publications, and once read Edgar Allan Poe's 'The Black Cat' to a garden full of drunk young people at his local gay pub The Jolly Farmers. His first published work was a Top Tip in 'Viz' of which he is justifiably proud.

David Michael Brown
David is a British ex-pat living in Sydney. Working as a freelance writer he has contributed to 'The Big Issue', 'TV Week', 'GQ', 'Rolling Stone' and 'Empire Magazine Australia', where he was Senior Editor for almost eight years. He is presently writing a book on the film music of German electronic music pioneers Tangerine Dream and researching the work of Andy Warhol associate and indie filmmaker Paul Morrissey for a forthcoming project.

Sebastian Corbascio
Sebastian is a writer/director and novelist. He was born and raised in Oakland Ca., and lives in Copenhagen, Denmark. His motion picture work can be seen on Youtube/Sebastian Corbascio. His murder mystery novel 'Sarah Luger' can be found on amazon.com. Reach him at facebook.com Sebastian Corbascio

Jonathon Dabell
Jonathon was born in Nottingham in 1976. He is a huge film fan and considers '70s cinema his favourite decade. He has written for 'Cinema Retro' and 'We Belong Dead', and co-authored 'More Than a Psycho: The Complete Films of Anthony Perkins' and 'Ultimate Warrior: The Complete Films of Yul Brynner' with his wife. He lives in Yorkshire with his wife, three kids, three cats and two rabbits!

John Harrison
John is a Melbourne, Australia-based freelance writer and film historian who has written for numerous genre publications, including 'Fatal Visions', 'Cult Movies', 'Is It Uncut?', 'Monster!' and 'Weng's Chop'. Harrison is also the author of the Headpress book 'Hip Pocket Sleaze: The Lurid World of Vintage Adult Paperbacks', has recorded audio commentaries for Kino Lorber, and composed the booklet essays for the Australian Blu-ray releases of *Thirst*, *Dead Kids* and *The Survivor*. 'Wildcat!', Harrison's book on the film and television career of former child evangelist Marjoe Gortner, was published by Bear Manor in 2020.

Rachel Bellwoar
Rachel is a writer for 'Comicon', 'Diabolique' magazine and 'Flickering Myth'. If she could have any director fim a biopic about her life it would be Aki Kaurismäki.

James Cadman
James first discovered his love of films as a child in the 1980s, happily scanning the shelves of his local video shop. Into his 20s, as part of his media degree, he secured work experience with a major film company which included visiting the set of *Notting Hill* at Shepperton Studios. Now living in Derbyshire with his wife and two young children, James enjoys watching and researching films, especially the '70s work of Eastwood, Friedkin, Peckinpah and Scorsese.

Dawn Dabell
Dawn runs her own clothing business in West Yorkshire. When she's not busy selling fabulous dresses and quirky tops, she's a full-time film enthusiast, writer and mum! She has written for 'Cinema Retro', 'We Belong Dead', 'Monster!' and 'Weng's Chop', and is also the co-author of 'More Than a Psycho: The Complete Films of Anthony Perkins' (2018) and 'Ultimate Warrior: The Complete Films of Yul Brynner' (2019). She is also the co-creator and designer of the very magazine you're holding in your hands right now.

David Flack
David was born and bred in Cambridge. Relatively new to the writing game, he has had reviews published in 'We Belong Dead' and 'Cinema of the '70s'. He loves watching, talking, reading and writing about film and participating on film forums. The best film he has seen in over 55 years of watching is *Jaws* (1975). The worst is *The Creeping Terror* (1963) or anything by Andy Milligan.

Darren Linder
Darren grew up in the '70s and has been forever enamored with films from that decade. He is a lifelong resident of Oregon, currently living in Portland. He has performed in many rock bands, ran a non-profit dog rescue, and worked in social service with at-risk youths. Currently he works security in music venues, and is completing a book about his experiences there to be published later this year. His favorite film directors of the '80s are John Carpenter, Brian De Palma and James Cameron.

Brian J. Robb

Brian is the 'New York Times' and 'Sunday Times' bestselling biographer of Leonardo Di Caprio, Keanu Reeves, Johnny Depp and Brad Pitt. He has also written books on silent cinema, the films of Philip K. Dick, horror director Wes Craven, classic comedy team Laurel and Hardy, the *Star Wars* movies, Superheroes, Gangsters, Walt Disney and the science fiction television series *Doctor Who* and *Star Trek*. His illustrated books include a History of Steampunk and an award-winning guide to J.R.R. Tolkien's Middle-earth. A former magazine and newspaper editor, he was co-founder of the Sci-Fi bulletin website and lives near Edinburgh.

Aaron Stielstra

Aaron was born in Ann Arbor, Michigan and grew up in Tucson, AZ and NYC. He is an actor, writer, director, soundtrack composer and illustrator. Since moving to Italy in 2012, he has appeared in spaghetti westerns, numerous crime movies, and horror-thrillers - most of them very wet - and recently completed the punk-rock comedies Weber Falls, USA and Excretion: the Shocking True Story of the Football Mom. He can be seen performing in his band War, Covid & Trump. His favorite '80s actor is Willem Dafoe.

Dr. Andrew C. Webber

Dr. W, a film teacher and examiner for over 35 years, already writes passionately for 'Cinema of the '70s' magazine and also contributes to the cassette gazette fanzine. He pontificates about music on the Low Noise podcast (available on Apple and Spotify) and his blogs can occasionally be found on Oxford's Ultimate Picture Palace cinema website. He still loves being "at" the movies and would describe himself as a lover of cinema, if asked.

Peter Sawford

Peter was born in Essex in 1964 so considers himself a child of the '70s. A self-confessed film buff, he loves watching, reading about and talking about cinema. A frustrated writer his whole life, he's only recently started submitting what he writes to magazines. His favourite director is Alfred Hitchcock with Billy Wilder running him a close second. He still lives in Essex with his wife and works as an IT trainer and when not watching films he's normally panicking over who West Ham are playing next.

Ian Taylor

Ian dabbled in horror fiction in the early '90s before writing and editing music fanzines. He later adjudicated plays for the Greater Manchester Drama Federation but enjoys film analysis most. Over the last five years, he has become a regular writer and editorial team member for 'We Belong Dead' magazine and contributed to all their book releases. This has led to writing for Dez Skinn's 'Halls of Horror', Allan Bryce's 'Dark Side' and Hemlock's 'Fantastic Fifties', amongst others. His first solo book 'All Sorts of Things Might Happen: The Films of Jenny Agutter' was recently released as a We Belong Dead publication.

Steven West

Steven's first published work was as a floppy haired teenager, voice breaking as he scribbled about Terence Fisher for an early issue of 'We Belong Dead' - a useful break from the lingerie section of the Freeman's catalogue. He still writes for the magazine and its spin offs while regularly contributing to 'The Fantastic Fifties' magazine and the UK Frightfest website, alongside www.horrorscreamsvideovault. co.uk. In 2019, Auteur Publishing released his 'Devil's Advocate' book about Wes Craven's *Scream*. Steven lives in Norfolk with his partner, daughter and - thanks to permanent home working - a dozen sock-puppet 'friends'.

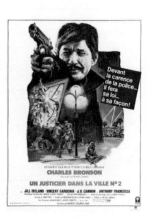

Printed in Great Britain
by Amazon